30TH ANNIVERSARY

CLASSIC *f*M

PUZZLE
BOOK

First published in Great Britain in 2022 by Cassell,
an imprint of Octopus Publishing Group Ltd
Carmelite House
50 Victoria Embankment
London EC4Y 0DZ
www.octopusbooks.co.uk

An Hachette UK Company
www.hachette.co.uk

All puzzles created by The Puzzle House.

ISBN 978-1-78840-408-2

A CIP catalogue record for this book is available from the British Library.

Printed and bound in the United Kingdom.

1 3 5 7 9 10 8 6 4 2

Publisher: Trevor Davies
Senior Editor: Leanne Bryan
Senior Designer: Jaz Bahra
Designer: Jeremy Tilston
Senior Production Manager: Katherine Hockley

This FSC® label means that materials used for the product have
been responsibly sourced.

30TH ANNIVERSARY

CLASSIC *f*M

PUZZLE BOOK

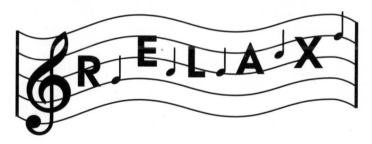

MINDFUL PUZZLES TO
RELAX AND UNWIND

FOREWORD BY
ALAN TITCHMARSH

C CASSELL

CONTENTS

FOREWORD   7

PUZZLES

GENTLE PUZZLES   11

MODERATE PUZZLES   75

CHALLENGING PUZZLES   139

SOLUTIONS

GENTLE SOLUTIONS   203

MODERATE SOLUTIONS   231

CHALLENGING SOLUTIONS   259

NOTES   286

FOREWORD

BY ALAN TITCHMARSH

My friends tell me I am a repository of astonishing facts. I think they are being rather kind. I call it having a dustbin mind. There is little rhyme or reason about the things I remember – not all of them useful – except that they must clearly have touched some kind of nerve when I first heard them, and amused me into retaining them. There are countless areas where my memory is a complete void – digits remain a puzzle to me and as a result I find it difficult to retain more than half a dozen telephone numbers. Perhaps, deep down, I know that all my family and friends are on speed dial and there is no reason to bother storing information that I can find at the push of a button. And numbers are so boring...

But words and facts. Ah, words are a completely different kettle of fish. I came top of the class at school in spelling (but at absolutely nothing else), which is of little consolation now when everyone has 'spellchecker' at their disposal. Still, at the time it offered me some consolation when I was third from the bottom in maths.

The fact that my English teacher was taken aback when I knew what 'reciprocated' meant and could spell 'separate', 'possession' and 'embarrassment' gave me a sudden glimpse of the power that words offer the user, along with little bits of knowledge that are not exactly the norm. I forget how long ago it was that I discovered that 'peristeronic' means 'of or relating to pigeons' and that if you take the first two letters of Dvořák's Christian name and the last four letters of his surname you come up with a word that tells you that his hobby was trainspotting: Anorak. I know. Excruciating.

When it comes to music, those who do not know me cannot understand why a gardener (and a writer, television and radio presenter, let's be fair) should know anything about music. Well, I have always sung, ever since childhood, in the church choir, and my taste is for the classical repertoire and musicals – a varied mix. I met my future wife in an operatic society – I sang and she danced. I know the operettas of Franz Lehár and Ivor Novello (few would now admit to that) and can be transported by the works of John Rutter and Ronald Binge (not obvious bedfellows). Listeners to my Saturday morning programme on Classic FM will also know that I like quizzing them with my weekly 'Titchmarsh Teaser', sometimes connected to music, sometimes not.

I cannot recall the number of times I have been invited onto Celebrity Mastermind but have always declined since I know that serendipity would no doubt result in my receiving questions that are way off-piste in terms of my knowledge. Of sport and pop music I know little. But on the works of P G Wodehouse and the music of Noël Coward I might do quite well. Quiz nights I love, and in the company of three other friends with a diverse range of specialist subjects l feel more comfortable, so l am delighted to be able to provide a foreword for this unputdownable puzzle book.

Puzzles delight and frustrate us in equal measure. How many times have you tried to recall the name of an actor, only to find yourself going though the alphabet in your head until a particular letter triggers the answer? That's me.

Whether l am listening to Tim Lihoreau on Classic FM while l am shaving in the morning, or Anne-Marie Minhall in the afternoon, or Andrew Collins on a Saturday evening playing film soundtracks, l will usually learn some fact that amuses or entertains and that l will hope to store away – probably in case it comes up in a quiz, or when l have the opportunity to dazzle the assembled company at supper around a kitchen table when the conversation has a lull. All of which might make me sound like a bit of a nerd.

l do hope not. I'm just someone who finds disparate facts and assorted bits of information to be the seasoning of life. They might be inconsequential, but life needs stardust as well as solid information. l hope this puzzle book brightens your days and brings those spicey little classic facts that might amuse and entertain your friends to the front of your mind. Use them wisely; for goodness sake don't bore the pants off them.

ALAN TITCHMARSH MBE

GENTLE
PUZZLES

1 KEY-BOARD

mn		A				mj		C
				D		mn	E	
E			B				F	
	E			mn	B		D	
G				E	C			B
	mj	mn		G			A	
	G		F	C		B		mn
	B	mj			G			
F						D		A

In this puzzle, each block of nine squares must contain the letters of the keys A, B, C, D, E, F and G, along with mj to denote a major key and mn to denote a minor key. Every row (going across) and every column (going down) must contain nine different keys.

2 MINDFULNESS

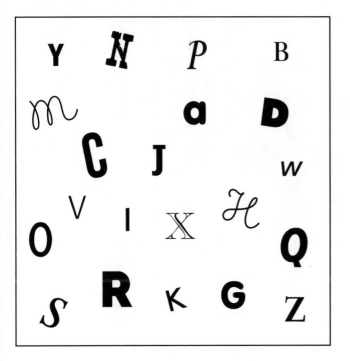

To solve this puzzle you need to use what you cannot see. Focus your mind on the letters of the alphabet that do NOT appear in the box. Use each missing letter once to form the name of a musical instrument.

3 EASE INTO EIGHT

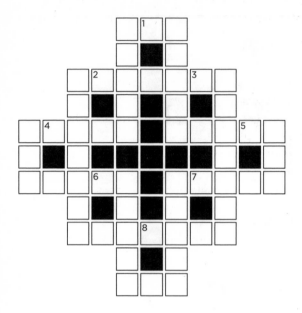

GENTLE PUZZLES

Solve the eight clues to find the eight-letter answers. The first letter of the answer goes in the numbered square in the grid, and the answer can go clockwise or anti-clockwise. You must work out which direction it goes.

Clues

1   Public musical performances
2   Type of guitar that has an amplifier or speaker, not acoustic
3   Three-sided percussion instrument
4   Acknowledgement of an excellent performance
5   Traditional piece of music telling a tale (4,4)
6   High female voices, and members of a family in a US crime drama series
7   Style of Spanish music and dance
8   Nationality of George Gershwin, born in Brooklyn, New York

4 IN THE SHADE

Take a break in the shade with this puzzle, based on a quotation by composer Claude Debussy.

Debussy was staying in Eastbourne to escape the scandal of his divorce. He complained that there were 'too many draughts and too much music...'. What did he go on to say?

Solve the clues and put the answers horizontally in the upper grid. They all have seven letters. Take the letters in the shaded squares from each answer and place them vertically in the lower grid to reveal how the quotation ends.

Clues

1   Now part of the Czech Republic, this region is associated with composer Smetana
2   The Orlando Symphony Orchestra is in this US state
3   A group of four musicians
4   First name of composer Strauss, shared with three English kings
5   A child with exceptional musical ability
6   City of Northern Ireland where flautist James Galway hails from
7   Currently employed, as in the music industry
8   Venue for performing live music
9   Asked specifically to join a company
10   Lead an orchestra with the baton

5 **LENTO**

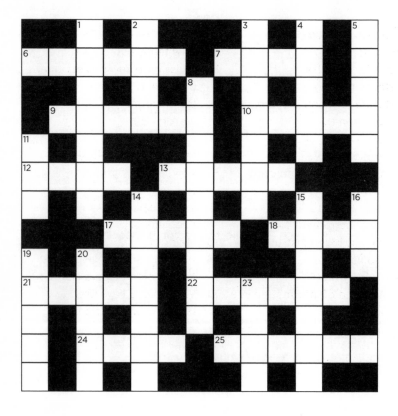

A no-tricks crossword.

Across

6 Goes before bass (6)
7 Prima donna (4)
9 Shout for an extra performance (6)
10 Yorkshire city, home of a piano competition (5)
12 A grass, or part of a mouthpiece (4)
13 Seen on a piano or a bicycle (5)
17 Musical play (5)
18 Stringed instrument (4)
21 Another stringed instrument – or a flower! (5)
22 Patriotic hymn (6)
24 Single piece of information in a programme (4)
25 Waltz suggesting it lasted only 60 seconds (6)

Down

1 Five performers (7)
2 Low female voice (4)
3 Swiss hero Tell, subject of an overture (7)
4 Home country of Katherine Jenkins (5)
5 Metal that gives its name to a group of instruments (5)
8 A practice for a performance (9)
11 Creative skill (3)
14 Amplifier (7)
15 Melodious (7)
16 Abbreviation of New York's Metropolitan Opera House (3)
19 What piano keys used to be made from, now banned (5)
20 A film (5)
23 Band of three (4)

6 CHILL OUT

The letters that appear in the word CHILL have been removed from the names of various musical instruments. Replace the letters and complete the names.

1 _ O N _ E R T _ N A

2 _ A R M O N _ _ A

3 _ _ A R _ N E T

4 P _ _ _ O _ O

5 _ _ _ M E S

6 _ E _ _ O

7 TIME LAG

A church choir is preparing for a concert of soothing choral classics. The choir is open to all ages. The youngest singer is Millie. Her mother, Sandra, also sings in the choir. She is four times as old as her daughter. Millie works out that in exactly 20 years she will be half as old as her mother will be then.

How old are Millie and Sandra now?

8 **LET GO**

Look at the words below. Follow the instructions to let go of some of the words to reveal the title of a piece of music.

1 PAVLOVA BEAR MELBA TRICOLOUR

2 CUCKOO HILL LARK NIGHTINGALE

3 CAT ANTHEM FLUTE HEADLAND

4 MOUNTAIN AIR SHARP TRIPOD

5 DITTY PEAK TOR LAKE

6 MOUSE HYMN ARIA THORN

7 MONKEY TRIO TIGER TRIANGLE

8 TRIPLET SWAN ORGANISE LION

Instructions

1 Let go of all the birds in row 2.
2 Let go of any words that mean a type of song.
3 Let go of any words that mean somewhere high up.
4 Let go of any words connected to the number three.
5 Let go of any words that contain a musical instrument.
6 Let go of the names of music-related people with a dessert named after them.
7 Let go of any mammals.

9 SOFTLY

P	I	A	N	O	L	A	C	E	L	U	A
A	E	P	E	D	A	L	X	D	J	P	O
S	P	R	Y	J	A	Z	P	U	P	P	V
T	O	T	C	P	A	R	T	L	M	Z	E
O	P	U	S	U	A	E	A	E	F	P	T
R	E	B	E	C	S	U	T	R	I	E	R
A	R	A	T	O	S	S	P	P	N	S	A
L	A	I	P	E	H	L	I	I	G	A	L
E	C	M	O	N	A	R	P	O	S	R	U
E	O	G	G	Y	R	S	A	J	N	H	P
C	G	R	O	U	P	X	R	Y	O	P	O
P	R	E	S	T	O	L	O	C	C	I	P

P is the musical sign for *piano*, meaning the music should be played softly. Find the names of musical words containing the letter *p* in the word square. All the words are in straight lines that run horizontally, vertically or diagonally. They may read forwards or backwards.

APPLAUSE
CLAP
COMPOSE
GROUP
OPERA
OPUS
PART
PASTORAL

PEDAL
PERCUSSION
PHRASE
PIANOLA
PICCOLO
PIPE
PLAY
POPULAR

PRACTICE
PRELUDE
PRESTO
RAP
SHARP
SOPRANO
SPINET
TEMPO

10 **DUOS**

Paul, George and Nigel are three tenors. Paula, Georgina and Nigella are three sopranos. They form three duos for a concert of romantic operatic arias.

Paula goes to sing before Nigel. Nigella is not the last soprano to sing. None of the men partners a woman with the female version of his own name.

Match the couples and give the order in which they sing.

11 MISSING FROM THE MOVIES

The vowels in these movie titles have been removed. Put them back to reveal the names of movies that have some of the best film scores of all time.

1 W S T S D S T R Y (three words)

2 L S M S R B L S (two words)

3 T T N C

4 L D S N L V N D R (three words)

5 T H G R T S C P (three words)

12 **STAR GAZING**

Seven stars of the music world have had the letters in their surnames rearranged in alphabetical order. Write the names vertically in the grid so that the shaded diagonal squares spell out the name of a famous ballet.

1	2	3	4	5	6	7

1 A D E G N R R
2 A D E I I N U
3 I I N O R S S
4 A A B E G T T
5 A D I I L V V
6 C E I L L O R
7 A D E N O S W

13 NUMBER NAMES

Each letter has been given a numerical value from 1 to 5. The total value of each word is reached by adding up the individual letters. No two letters have the same number.

A I R = 6

I D A = 10

A I D A = 13

R A D I O = 15

What is the individual value of each letter?

14 **CLOUD NINE**

Each number from 1 to 9 represents a different letter of the alphabet. Solve the clues and write the letters in the appropriate spaces in the grid to reveal a word linked to the discipline of learning and playing music.

1	2	3	4	5	6	7	8	9

Clues

a)	Ribbon inside a cassette cartridge	5 3 1 8
b)	Performers collectively in a show	4 3 7 5
c)	Be in charge of a production, but not on stage	9 6 2 8 4 5

15 BEHIND THE SCENES

Which composers are hiding behind the scenes in the sentences below? Discover them by joining words or parts of words together.

1 Whenever I travel, gardens and concerts are at the top of my wish list.
2 Ruth and Eleanor sang the famous *Flower Duet* from *Lakme*.
3 The music impresario arrived in his Cadillac. Hop in, he said, so we all did.
4 The range of music performed, stretched over different eras and genres.

16 HAVE A BREAK

The letters in the two-word names of pieces of music have been split and rearranged into a line. The letters remain in the correct order for each word. In each case, both words in the title have the same number of letters. Can you work out the titles?

1 S L A W K A N E

2 P E G Y E R N T

3 W M A T U E S I R C

17 **WHAT AM I?**

My first is in NOTES
And isn't in TONE.
My second's in CHAT
And also in PHONE.
My third is in PLAY
And also in HEAR.
My fourth is in BRIGHT
And also in CLEAR.
My fifth is in PACE
And also in POUND.
Do you know what I do?
I change a note's sound.

18 **BLOWING BUBBLES**

There are three bubbles and three words to be formed. The question mark stands for a mystery letter, which appears in all three words. Use all the letters in each bubble once, including the mystery letter, to find the words.

You are looking for three types of professional musician.

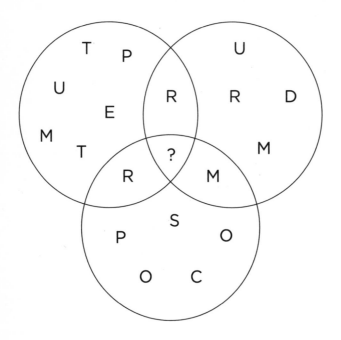

19 HALF FULL?

Is your glass half full or half empty? The following puzzle calls for positive thinking.

The clues below are listed at random, but they each have a four-letter answer. Solve the clues, then write the words in the grid so that the last two letters of one answer become the first two letters of the next. Each first letter appears in a numbered space.

1		2		3		4		5			

Clues

Play at different venues with a musical performance
A campanologist will create one
A reverberated sound
A low female voice
What is missing? *Land of_____ and Glory*

20 **RING CYCLE**

Solve the clues, which are in no particular order, and slot the seven-letter answers into their correct places in the ring. The last letter of one answer forms the first letter of the next. Answer 1 begins with a letter S.

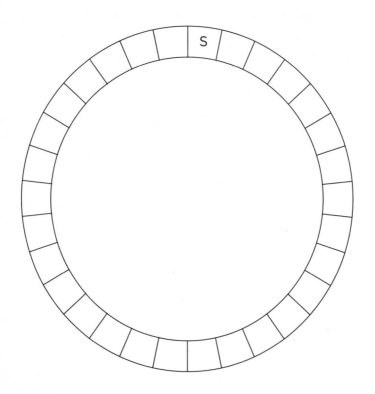

Clues

The name of a Beethoven concerto shared with the largest breed of penguin

Chorus

East Anglian coastal county, birthplace of Benjamin Britten

Styluses, which follow the grooves on a record player

Singing against a pre-recorded backing track

21 SMOOTHIE

Simon is in need of a serious musical chill out, listening to his favourite smooth classics.

He has set aside a whole day to unwind with the music.

He starts off with half an hour of guitar favourites and finishes his day with three hours of Gregorian chant. In total, 40% of his day is spent listening to piano concertos and a quarter of his day is spent enjoying music written for the violin.

How many hours has Simon spent listening to music?

22 HALL OF FAME

The Classic FM Hall of Fame is the most comprehensive classical chart in the world, as the Top 300 is decided by votes from listeners. There are surprises every year, with unexpected chart rises, unpredicted downturns of fortune and exciting new entries.

Imagine a Top 300 where the following things have happened.

130 records have moved up the chart from last time. That is five times the number of new entries. One in ten records in the chart is a non-mover, occupying the same chart placing as the previous year.

How many records in the Top 300 are on their way *down* the chart?

23 PERFECT FIFTH

Solve the clues, which are listed at random. Each answer contains five letters. Complete the grid so that each answer starts in a space with an odd number and ends in the space with the even number that is one greater. To give you a perfect start, the letter in space 1 is M.

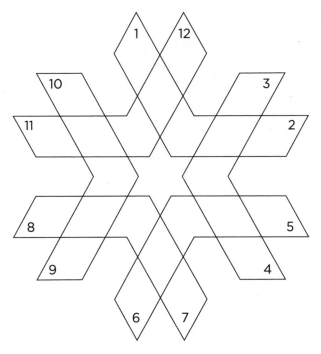

Clues
Not pieces of eight, but this eight play pieces
Outspoken with regard to voice
Appear to toast rum and play guitar
Military music this month
Wins over rhythms
Music teacher pickled trout

24 SIXTH SENSE

All answers have six letters. 1 to 6 start in the outer circle and are written towards the centre. 7 to 12 go round the rings in a clockwise direction.

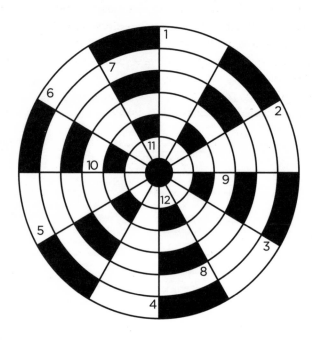

Questions
1 Which famous conductor has the same name as a baby's toy?
2 Which word means 'acquired knowledge' – musical or otherwise?
3 What is a cast of performers also known as?
4 Which of Holst's planets is said to have rings around it?
5 Where are musical recordings made?
6 What can mean the level of sound in music or a music book?
7 What name is given to a musician's whole professional life?
8 What is a military musical marching entertainment called?
9 What will you have done if you waited in line to buy tickets?
10 Which instrument is played by strumming and plucking?
11 If you are in the spotlight, you are said to be where on stage?
12 What does an audience call out if they want more?

25 **HONEYCOMB**

All answers have six letters and fit into the grid in a clockwise direction. The first letter of the answer to Clue 1 is given (F) but after that you'll have to work out in which hexagonal cell the answer begins.

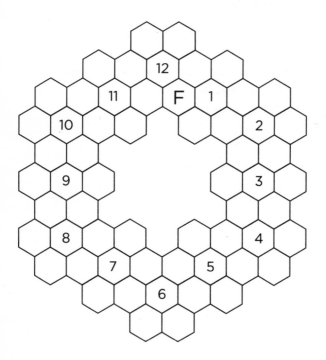

GENTLE PUZZLES

Clues

1   The last part of a piece of work
2   Someone who performs on a musical instrument
3   Religious role that completes this coronation anthem, *Zadok the*
    _____
4   Building such as the Victoria and Albert, where musical instruments may be displayed
5   Produced a tune with sealed lips
6   Describes Isata age-wise in the Kanneh-Mason siblings
7   L stands for this in LSO, the oldest surviving orchestra in this city
8   A tune
9   Italian city, described as Neapolitan, with a rich music history
10 Moved to steps in a waltz or paso doblo, for example
11 Another name for the violin
12 Famous tower in the French city know for L'Opera, founded in 1669

26 **TAKE NOTE**

Each letter that appears in the treble clef (A, B, C, D, E, F and G) has been replaced by a musical note. The other letters of the alphabet are in place. Work out the words then match them up to find the names of three two-word musical instruments.

♪ O U ♪ L ♪

♪ N ♪ L ♪ I S

♪ L ♪ ♪ T R I ♪

♪ ♪ S S

♪ O R

♪ U I T ♪ R

27 **CAR RIDE**

Solve the quickfire clues below to find answers that all contain the word 'car'. It might appear at the beginning of the word, in the middle or at the end.

1   Academy Award
2   Bright floor covering for a privileged guest (3,6)
3   Opera first performed in 1875
4   Italian tenor who achieved great acclaim at Covent Garden in the early years of the 20th century
5   Flower worn by Sir Malcolm Sargent whenever he conducted the Proms
6   *The Sorcerer's Apprentice* featured in a Mickey Mouse _____

28 TO THE POINT

Each answer contains four letters. The first letter goes in a numbered triangle, the second letter directly above it, the third letter to the right and the fourth to the left.

Clues

1   An opera company's series of performances in country-wide venues
2   Word that follows *Born* in the name of the 1966 movie with soundtrack by John Barry
3   A melody
4   A vote that might block a decision in a singing contest, for example
5   A screen _____ assesses a performer's suitability for a film role
6   Concludes, finishes
7   Capital city of the country where Luciano Pavarotti was born
8   Something on a list of pieces outlined in a music programme
9   Enya comes from what is said to be the Emerald one
10 The object of a fan's affections

29 **TAKE FIVE**

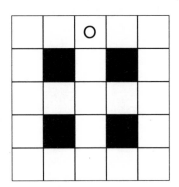

Solve the musical clues, which are listed at random. All the answers contain five letters. Fit the answers in the grid, going either across or down. There is a starter letter to help you on the way. There is only one way to fit all the words in the grid.

Clues
Group of singers rehearsing together
Woodwind instruments
Main characters in a theatrical production
Religious song performed in December
Madame Butterfly for example
Short breaks written in a piece of music

30 **FILLERS**

In each group, find a single music-linked word to fill the spaces and complete the longer words.

1 S _ _ _ _ S
   B A R I _ _ _ _
   A _ _ _ _ D

2 R E _ _ _ _
   _ _ _ _ G R O U N D
   D I S _ _ _ _

3 E L _ _ _
   _ _ _ L I N G
   _ _ _ L E R

31 **COMPOSE YOURSELF**

1						
2	E					
3						
4						
5				I		
6						
7						

You need to stay calm and composed for this puzzle!

Place all the seven-letter music-linked words below in the grid in the right order to reveal the name of a famous contemporary composer. The two vowels in his surname are already in place.

BERLIOZ
BUSKING
EINAUDI
HARMONY
JANACEK
OCTAVES
PUCCINI

32 BAX WORDS

The name of a composer is hidden in the sentences below, but it has been written backwards. Look for a continuous line of letters from right to left to spell out a composer's surname. Arnold Bax isn't to be found!

1   There is deep chasm harbouring a wide difference in the quality of singing.
2   We tried to return to our hotel after the opera but each cab in the area was taken.
3   On a music tour of California, visits to the notorious island of Alcatraz omitted much of its frightening history.
4   This new opera puts *Lohengrin* in the shade.

33 **MOVIE A TO Z**

Here are the names of some movies with music that has featured in the Classic FM Hall of Fame. The letters are shown in alphabetical order. Rearrange them to find the movie titles.

1 D E I L W

2 E H I I M N O S S T (two words)

3 A A C E E E E G H P R S T T (three words)

4 A A D G I L O R T

34 MY MISTAKE

Chaos and confusion reign in the publicity office, which has resulted in errors on the posters advertising the film club's new programme. It's only one wrong letter, but it creates a new word and gives the film title a whole new meaning! From the clues, work out the incorrect titles and what they should really be.

Clues

1 Part of a very highly rated hospital   (two words)
2 Lost and isolated in Italy's capital   (two words)
3 Completely devoted follower of a sports or entertainment star

35 **REARRANGEMENT**

There are two clues to help you find two solutions. The first clue leads you to a general word. The second clue leads you to the name of a composer. You will need all your skills as an arranger, as the second word is an anagram of the first – it has all the same letters, but in a different order.

1 Paved approach to a house
Italian writer of opera, including *Aida* and *Rigoletto*

2 Very big
Famous for *Land of Hope and Glory*

3 Useful and practical
Austrian composer of over 100 operas; his name sounds as though he wants to be concealed!

4 Found on a door or a saucepan
His *Messiah* is a popular choral work

5 Equine animal
Composer with a name that suggests the sea who created the music for *The Hobbit*

36 **LUCKY NUMBERS**

Test your musical knowledge and your basic arithmetic skills in one puzzle.

1   What do you get if you multiply the date in July in the Tom Cruise movie that has a John Williams soundtrack, and the number who are *Magnificent* in the 1960 classic?

2   What do you get if you multiply the number of the year in the sci-fi movie that has Strauss's *Also Sprach Zarathustra* as its soundtrack, and the number of New York gangs there are in *West Side Story*?

3   What do you get if you multiply the number of performers in a sestet, by the number of different letters of the alphabet there are on a piano keyboard?

4   What do you get if you multiply the number of turtle doves delivered on the second day of Christmas, by the number of performers in three trios?

37 MUSIC BOX

Y	F	T	O	M	T
X	L	L	D	J	T
Q	A	O	Y	S	N
A	T	C	E	R	Q
G	U	T	E	D	E
S	T	R	A	S	Z

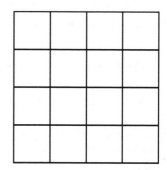

In a word square, the same words can be read both across and down. Your challenge is to create a musical word square in the empty grid using the four music-related words hidden in the letter box. The words in the letter box all appear in straight lines that can go in any direction. They all contain four letters.

CLUE: One word is the name of a stringed musical instrument.

38 FORWARD PLANNING

There are two clues to help you find two solutions. The first clue leads you to a general word. The second clue leads you to a music-based word. The solutions are very similar, but in the second word the middle letter has moved *forwards* in the alphabet.

1   Piece of furniture to sit on
Group of singers

2   Nobleman
Stick used by an orchestral conductor

3   The Society of Friends, known for its pacifism and educational work
Notes with half the value of crotchets

4   Thin biscuit eaten with ice cream
Piece by Handel for performing on the Thames for George I,
The _____ Music

39 IN MY LIFETIME

Look at these important events. What year did they take place?
Decide which of the three performers listed was alive at the time.

1 The year England won the football World Cup.
In whose lifetime did this event take place?
a)   Alexander Armstrong
b)   Aled Jones
c)   Bryn Terfel

2 The year the Channel Tunnel opened.
In whose lifetime did this event take place?
a)   Nicola Benedetti
b)   Jess Gillam
c)   Sheku Kanneh-Mason

3 The year that *The Good, the Bad and the Ugly* was released.
In whose lifetime did this event take place?
a)   Alfie Boe
b)   Nigel Kennedy
c)   Freddie de Tommaso

40 **MAJOR SEVENTH**

The classical music-related words below all contain seven letters. Put them in the grid either across or down. There is only one way to fit all the words in. One letter has been given to start you off.

BERLIOZ
CADENCE
CADENZA
DELIBES
FANTASY
IRELAND
ITALIAN
SCHERZO
SOLOIST
TIPPETT
TRUMPET
VIOLINS

41 **WISE WORDS**

Your challenge is to work out the hidden quotation by a composer describing a work by fellow composer Anton Webern.

Solve the clues and put the eight-letter answers horizontally in the first grid. Reading downwards, column A will reveal the name of the composer.

Use the first grid to help you complete the second one by putting in the letters that correspond to the grid coordinates. The completed second grid will reveal the quotation describing Webern's work.

	A	B	C	D	E	F	G	H
1								
2								
3								
4								
5								
6								
7								
8								
9								
10								

GENTLE PUZZLES

Clues

1 Piece of music sung or played under a lady's window in the evening
2 Wind instrument played by Emma Johnson
3 Small chime held in the palm or with the fingers
4 Musician who plays a church instrument
5 Taking pleasure in a concert, for example
6 A piece of romantic music, played at night?
7 A low male voice
8 A group of musicians who play together
9 Gershwin wrote one in Blue!
10 Describes a deep, rough voice

F1		F2	B6	D10	F3	G8		D7	B5		C9	
E9	F5	E1	C4	H3	D8		A10	G2	C8	E7	E6	C1	H7
C2		C5	F9	H10		F4	C3		B7				
F8	F6	H1	B3	D6	B9							

42 INSTRUMENTS

```
T J H T L S A X O P H O N E M
T X L N A G O T G L Z T E S A
A I R R V B E L T U E R I J N
Y O M P B N O A L I I T M I D
H H M P I A Z R X E A T T M O
P Z T R A D S Q Y R C R A P L
Z I A R A N R S L O U M P R I
T L A L O J I O O M E A B G N
C E O N O M L E P O U T O T M
E I N R O O B E H N N Y U P E
V O G R C E T O O S I B T L N
X A E C O O R B N G A L G O F
N S I N B C O W E E N U O N Z
A P O U R E H T I Z B O H I E
H A R P S I C H O R D A G Y V
```

The names of a whole orchestra of musical instruments are hidden in the word square. All words are in straight lines that run horizontally, vertically or diagonally. They may read forwards or backwards.

BUGLE

CELLO

CLARINET

CORNET

FLUTE

GONG

GUITAR

HARPSICHORD

HORN

MANDOLIN

OBOE

ORGAN

PIANO

PICCOLO

SAXOPHONE

SITAR

TABOR

TIMPANI

TROMBONE

TRUMPET

TUBA

VIOLA

VIOLIN

XYLOPHONE

ZITHER

43 SILENT VOICES

The four voices that make up the four-part harmony in these vocal works have been replaced by question marks. Each question mark could be an S (soprano), A (alto), T (tenor) or B (bass). Work out the missing letters to identify the vocal works.

1 M E ? ? I ? H (Handel)

2 ? O ? C ? (Puccini)

3 ? I D ? (Verdi)

4 L ? C R I M O ? ? (Mozart)

5 ? V E M ? R I ? (Schubert)

44 **PROMISING SIGNS**

Music and astrology meet in in Debbie Wiseman's acclaimed *The Musical Zodiac*. In the musical pieces representing star signs below, the letters have been replaced by symbols.

PISCES is

What are the rest of the star signs in Wiseman's work?

1

2

3

4

5

45 **INNER CALM**

Solve the clues. Starting in the top left-hand square of the grid, write the answers moving inwards in a clockwise direction. The words overlap with *at least* the last letter of one answer becoming the first letter of the next answer. Calmly does it!

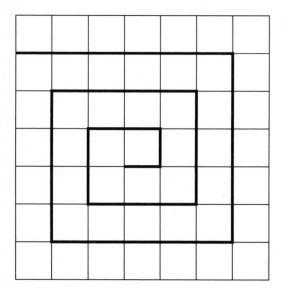

GENTLE PUZZLES

Clues

1 Katherine Jenkins is this type of performer
2 Film score by Howard Shore, *The Lord of the* _____
3 *Lullaby* by Whitacre including the title of an amphibious aquatic mammal
4 First name of the man who wrote the poems of *The Glorious Garden*
5 Saint-Saens wrote about *The Carnival* of which living creatures?
6 Full house, no tickets left! (two words)
7 New Zealand opera soprano Dame Kiri (two words)
8 Dancing in triple time
9 Composer Philip, whose surname sounds like a wine goblet
10 Player or singer who performs alone

46 **CODA**

5		4		26	6	6	3	5	10	7	6	11
1 A	2 R	3 T	4 S		24		5		2		1	
2		1		15	25	1	20	26	1	9	17	
24	1	2	17	6	3		11		4		5	
10		21		20		17			2		1	
11	6	1	2	4		2	6	14	23	6	4	3
19		18		24	23	12			13		3	
4	16	6	6	3	6	11		15	19	6	9	6
6		2		4		24			2		11	
	8		4	4		19	11	7	6	11	3	
3	23	3	10	2	19	1	25		11		19	
	2		25	1		1		6	9	5	10	
22	20	25	10	15	5	10	11	6		6	11	

GENTLE PUZZLES

Each letter of the alphabet has been replaced by a number. Work out which number represents which letter to complete the crossword-style grid. Words can go across or down. One word has been given to start you off.

HINTS:
The letters in the word across the top row spell out a famous composer. The letters in the word across the bottom row spell out a musical instrument.
When you have cracked the code, the letters 24, 10, 10, 11, 25, 19, 21, 5, 3, 4, 10, 11, 1, 3, 1 spell out a piece of music from the composer above.

Fill in the grid below with the letters corresponding to each number as you discover them.

1	2	3	4	5	6	7	8	9	10	11	12	13
14	15	16	17	18	19	20	21	22	23	24	25	26

47 **PERSONAL CHOICE**

Ian has always wanted to play a keyboard instrument, and he has chosen the piano.

Leo has always wanted to play a string instrument, and he has chosen the cello.

Tia has always wanted to play an instrument with strings, and she has chosen the guitar.

Tom has always wanted to play a brass instrument. Which instrument has he chosen?

48 ADDERS

Each conundrum leads to a music-related word.

1   What do you get if you add a former US president to an alien?
2   What do you get if you add an old cloth to something measured by a clock?
3   What do you get if you add a vital accessory to tubing to carry water or gas?
4   What do you get if you add a door opener to a plank of wood?
5   Who do you get if you add Morecambe's partner to a grown boy?

49 E-E-EASY DOES IT

E is the most used letter in the English language, but there's not
a single letter E in all the surnames of composers listed below who
have graced the Classic FM Hall of Fame. Fit all the names into the
grid, across or down. E-e-easy does it!

4 letters
BACH   ORFF   PART

5 letters
BARRY   BRUCH   FINZI   GLASS   HOLST   HAYDN   PARRY   QUINN

6 letters
BRAHMS   CHOPIN   DVORAK   MOZART   TALLIS   WALTON   ZIPOLI

7 letters
BORODIN   COPLAND   PUCCINI   ROSSINI

8 letters
ALBINONI   GIURIOLI   KORNGOLD   MASCAGNI   SCHUMANN

9 letters
ARMSTRONG   PIAZZOLLA

11 letters
TCHAIKOVSKY

12 letters
RACHMANINOFF

15 letters
VAUGHAN WILLIAMS

50 **CRYPTIC**

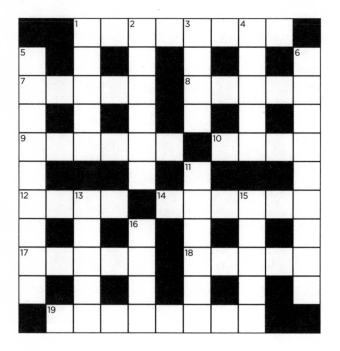

A cryptic crossword to massage the mind.

Across

1 Flat toes trodden on to give high voice (8)
7 Sounds like bread products play a part here (5)
8 Brendan certainly reveals his musical moves (5)
9 Shed to become what compere did at concert (6)
10 The three disturb riot (4)
12 Play a record by dividing a snip (4)
14 Song revealed at ball Adam attended (6)
17 Arise loudly and do this to the roof! (5)
18 The echo I responded to came from the singers apparently (5)
19 Shrill sounds from card game Les followed (8)

Down

1 Thinly coat movies (5)
2 Lend an ear to silent changes (6)
3 Send alternative finales (4)
4 Sounds like a money note for this vocalist (5)
5 Carthorse bolts in the direction of these musicians (9)
6 Data keepers for types of flute (9)
11 Can cellos apparently annul? (6)
13 Heir I should acknowledge as a musician from the Emerald Isle (5)
15 They have a pride in music from a Hans Zimmer soundtrack (5)
16 Locks piano notes (4)

MODERATE PUZZLES

51 KEY-BOARD

	G				D	mj		
E				G				
mn		C	mj					
			F				G	C
mj					mn			F
G	E		B					
			C			F		B
					E			mn
		mn		B			C	

In this puzzle, each block of nine squares must contain the letters of the keys A, B, C, D, E, F and G, along with mj to denote a major key and mn to denote a minor key. Every row (going across) and every column (going down) must contain nine different keys.

52 MINDFULNESS

To solve this puzzle you need to use what you cannot see. Focus your mind on the letters of the alphabet that do NOT appear in the box. Use each missing letter once to form the name of a composer.

53 **EASE INTO EIGHT**

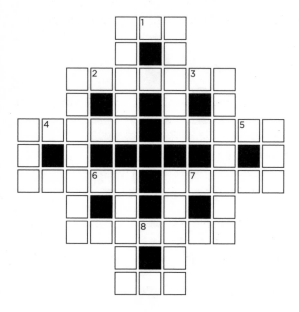

Solve the eight clues to find the eight-letter answers. The first letter of the answer goes in the numbered square in the grid, and the answer can go clockwise or anti-clockwise. You must work out which direction it goes.

Clues

1 Large percussion instrument, the largest of this group in the orchestra (4,4)
2 Woodwind instrument, once known as the fipple flute
3 Wind instrument that originated in Scotland
4 Work in which a solo instrument contrasts with the orchestra
5 Lighter type of vocal musical work made popular by Offenbach and Lehár
6 Austrian composer Franz, whose ninth symphony was 'Unfinished'
7 Instrument that evolved from the sackbut
8 Gilbert and Sullivan work, where fairies take over Parliament

54 **IN THE SHADE**

1						
2						
3						
4						
5						
6						
7						
8						
9						
10						

1	2	3	4	5	6	7	8	9	10

Take a break in the shade with this puzzle, based on a quotation by composer Igor Stravinsky. The quotation begins with the words, 'My music is best understood...'. How does it end?

Solve the clues and put the answers horizontally in the upper grid. They all have seven letters. Take the letters in the shaded squares from each answer and place them vertically in the lower grid to reveal how the quotation ends

Clues

1   Wooden musical instrument from the woodwind section of the orchestra
2   Performing, making music
3   Thin plastic discs that reproduce music
4   Composers Liszt and Bartók came from this country
5   Nationality of Sibelius
6   Sheku Kanneh-Mason is this type of musician
7   John Williams has been nominated for more than 50 _____ Awards
8   South American percussion instruments originally made from gourds
9   Small, four-stringed guitar from Hawaii
10 Brass instruments, in this case nothing to do with ice cream!

55 LENTO

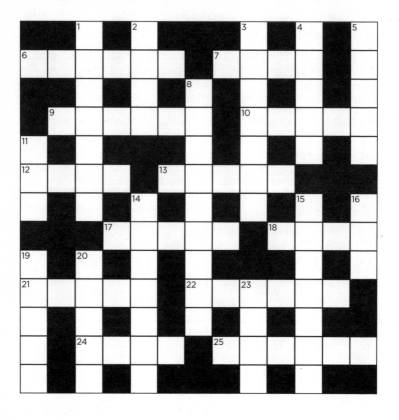

MODERATE PUZZLES

A no-tricks crossword.

Across

6 Singers, including sopranos, altos, tenors and basses (6)
7 Hollow metal instrument in the percussion section (4)
9 See 18 Across
10 Country that the sitar is from (5)
12 Finishes, concludes (4)
13 Home country of Luciano Pavarotti (5)
17 First name of composer Copland (5)
18 & 9 River made famous by Strauss in *The Beautiful* _____ _____ (4,6)
21 Dance music played to big band jazz (5)
22 & 5 Down Composer of the *Enigma Variations* (6,5)
24 Applaud (4)
25 _____ song, another name for a lullaby (6)

Down

1 Italian composer of *The Four Seasons* (7)
2 South American country famous for its traditional panpipes (4)
3 Home of Rossini's operatic *Barber* (7)
4 The telescopic joint of a trumpet, which shares its name with a piece of playground equipment (5)
5 See 22 Across
8 German composer whose Symphony No. 9 was the 'Choral' (9)
11 Dvořák composition, *From the _____ World* (3)
14 British composer Ralph _____ Williams (7)
15 Holiday state of south-eastern USA, where Delius worked in an orange grove (7)
16 It could be major or minor (3)
19 Sacred song (5)
20 Level of music sound, or a sports field (5)
23 A musical composition (4)

56 **CHILL OUT**

The letters that appear in the word CHILL have been removed from the names of various musical terms. Replace the letters and complete the terms.

1 _ A R _ _ _ O N

2 _ A P R _ _ _ _ O

3 _ _ R O M A T _ _

4 P _ T _ _

5 P _ A _ N _ _ A N T

6 O _ T A _ _ O R D

57 RETRO

At a retro music sale, Julie has taken a stall to sell off some of her old vinyl records. In the first few minutes, she sells three records. She also visits a stall selling musical scores. She purchases two items and finds that she has spent £2 more than she has taken.

The next hour is quiet and she only sells two records. On impulse, she goes and buys another score. Her outlay is still £2 more than she had taken.

Julie is determined that she will not buy anything else, and that she will end the day with a clear £20 profit.

All Julie's records are priced the same, as are all the music scores that she purchased.

How many more records must she sell?

58 SEARCH FOR CALM

```
R  I  S  N  E  Y  B  A  L  L  U  L
J  I  M  O  O  D  O  E  Z  M  O  E
E  T  T  E  S  A  H  N  U  D  D  O
C  S  J  A  E  T  C  T  N  A  I  M
O  Z  U  R  R  L  E  A  F  G  L  I
V  A  E  A  E  D  T  N  A  Y  E  S
O  S  N  G  R  N  A  D  U  L  N  S
T  N  A  D  E  R  A  N  G  T  T  I
T  T  A  L  A  R  G  O  D  F  O  N
O  B  L  I  W  N  E  C  L  O  D  A
S  A  H  A  P  G  T  R  I  S  H  I
R  D  I  M  I  N  U  E  N  D  O  P
```

Musical words linked with peace and calm are hidden in the word square. All words are in straight lines that run horizontally, vertically or diagonally. They may read forwards or backwards. There is one word in the list that is not in the word square. Which word is it?

ADAGIO
ANDANTE
DIMINUENDO
DOLCE
ECHO
FADE
HARMONY
LARGO
LEGATO
LENTO
LULLABY
MOOD
MUTE
PIANISSIMO
PIANO
RALLENTANDO
REST
RITARDANDO
SOFTLY
SOSTENUTO
SOTTO VOCE

59 LET GO

Look at the words below. Follow the instructions to let go of some of the words to reveal the title of a piece of music.

	A	B	C	D
1	Sousa	waltz	five	tango
2	cello	zither	eight	guitar
3	Bliss	Mozart	Rossini	Britten
4	seasons	kazoo	Sax	viola
5	polka	jive	six	wedding
6	lute	bazooka	anniversary	rumba
7	Wagner	Chopin	seven	Moog
8	Bartók	Liszt	four	birthday

1 Let go of any people who have instruments named after them.
2 Let go of composers in row 3 who have an l in their name.
3 Let go of any musical instruments in column B that contain a Z.
4 Let go of any stringed instruments.
5 Let go of any number that has a different value from the number of letters in its name.
6 Let go of all dances.
7 Let go of any celebrations.
8 Let go of composers in columns A and B.

60 **HAPPY BIRTHDAY**

Members of the local choir love to send each other birthday cards. Everyone sends an individual card to every other member of the choir, not forgetting a card to the music director. The music director feels he is above this sort of thing so he does not send any cards out, even though he receives a card from every individual in the choir. There are twice as many ladies as gentlemen in the choir. In total, 225 cards are sent in a single year.

How many people are in the choir?

61 **MISSING FROM THE MOVIES**

The vowels in these movie titles have been removed. Put them back to reveal the names of movies that have some of the best film scores of all time.

1 S V N G P R V T R Y N (three words)

2 R D R S F T H L S T R K (five words)

3 H M L N (two words)

4 W R H R S (two words)

5 W R F T H W R L D S (four words)

They are all written by the same composer. Who is he?

62 STAR GAZING

Seven words with a musical link (instrument, performer, performance) have had their letters rearranged in alphabetical order. Write the names vertically in the grid so that the shaded diagonal squares spell out the surname of a British composer.

1	2	3	4	5	6	7

1 E H I L S T W
2 C C I L O O P
3 A B N O O S S
4 A E L M N S T
5 D E M M R R U
6 A C E I L R T
7 A E F I N R R

63 **NUMBER NAMES**

Each letter has been given a numerical value from 1 to 7. The total value of each word is reached by adding up the individual letters. No two letters have the same number.

P O E M = 10

M O R E = 15

P R O M = 16

M U T E = 16

T E M P O = 16

What is the value of T R U M P E T ?

64 **CLOUD NINE**

Each number from 1 to 9 represents a different letter of the alphabet. Solve the clues and write the letters in the appropriate spaces in the grid to reveal a two-word phrase related to traditional music.

1	2	3	4	5	6	7	8	9

Clues

a) Performance by one person	9 2 3 2
b) Woodwind instrument	1 3 6 5 8
c) Solemn sound of a bell	4 7 8 3 3

65 BEHIND THE SCENES

Which composers are hiding behind the scenes in the sentences below? Discover them by joining words or parts of words together.

1   A difficult piece for playing; luck was on his side, fortunately.
2   Music written for this sad tale harmonises beautifully with the words.
3   A famous composer is the model I usually focus my attention on.
4   The result of the singing competition is a tie for the first time ever.

66 HAVE A BREAK

The rows of letters below are each made up of two words which have been split and rearranged. The letters remain in the correct order for each word. In each case, both words have the same number of letters.

1 is the two-word name of an opera.
2 is the name of two different operas.
3 is the name of two characters from opera.

Can you work out what they are?

1   E O N E G U G E N I N E

2   L A T O K S C M A E

3   C F I A R G A M R E N O

67 WHAT AM I?

My first is in REST
And also in DREAM.
My second's in WATER
And also in STREAM.
My third is in FIND
And also in HIDE.
My fourth is in SAIL
And also in GLIDE.
My fifth is in COMFORT
And also in GLOW.
I can help you to chill,
And take things so slow.

68 BLOWING BUBBLES

There are three bubbles and three words to be formed. The question mark stands for a mystery letter, which appears in all three words. Use all the letters in each bubble once, including the mystery letter, to find the words.

You are looking for the surnames of three classical singers.

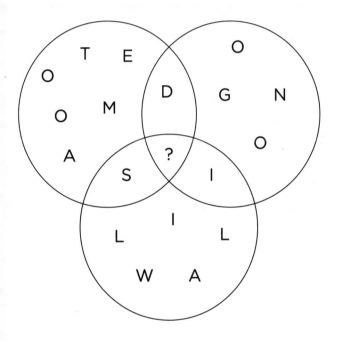

69 HALF FULL?

Is your glass half full or half empty? The following puzzle calls for positive thinking.

The clues below are listed at random, but they each have a four-letter answer. Solve the clues, then write the words in the grid so that the last two letters of one answer become the first two letters of the next. Each first letter appears in a numbered space.

1		2		3		4		5			

Clues

First name of Indian sitar virtuoso Shankar
Lady that the theme from the movie *Dr Zhivago* is named after
Home city of the Latvian National Symphony Orchestra
A celebratory performance or festival
Renaissance stringed instrument

70 **RING CYCLE**

Solve the clues, which are in no particular order, and slot the seven-letter answers into their correct places in the ring. The last letter of one answer forms the first letter of the next. Answer 1 begins with a letter S.

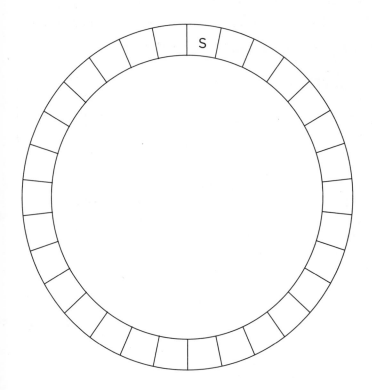

Clues

Shostakovich symphony dedicated *To an autumnal month*

Beats, accents, metres

Person who performs alone

Describes a movement in a lively tempo

A keyboard piece designed to show musical skill

71 SOUNDTRACK

A university course in video-game music has been busy producing soundtracks for movies created by other students. In descending order, these were voted the top soundtracks of all those submitted.

NEVER SAY NO NEVER

LAST WOMAN STANDING

DANCING WITH REELS AND JIGS

INFO URGENTLY NEEDED

What is unique about the result?

72 IN TRAINING

As well as vocal training and hours of work in the rehearsal room, a top diva needs to keep at her best physically. She has established a routine where she spends one day a week working out.

She leaves her home at 10 am and runs to the opera house. She then turns round without stopping and speed walks the same route, arriving back home at 3 pm.

Her average running speed is 6 miles per hour.
Her average speed walking speed is 4 miles per hour.

How far does she live from the opera house?

73 PERFECT FIFTH

Solve the clues, which are listed at random. Each answer contains five letters. Complete the grid so that each answer starts in a space with an odd number and ends in the space with the even number that is one greater. To give you a perfect start, the letter in space 1 is V.

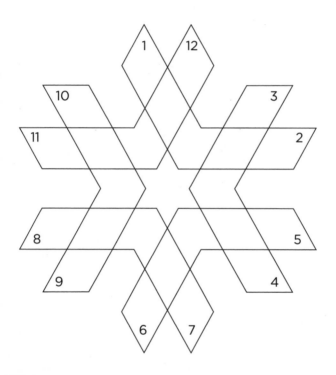

Clues

Significant key

It invigorates the first degree of a scale

Rewrite Puccini opera at this racecourse

Regal change for composer

Stringed instrument in hanging basket

Remove queen from gun holder to discover planets creator

74 TAKE NOTE

Each letter that appears in the treble clef (A, B, C, D, E, F and G) has been replaced by a musical note. The other letters of the alphabet are in place. Work out the words then match them up to find the names of three composers and their compositions.

OR ♪ ♪

S I ♪ ♪ ♪ R I ♪ ♪

V ♪ R ♪ I

♪ ♪ R M I N ♪   ♪ U R ♪ N ♪

W ♪ ♪ N ♪ R

♪ I ♪ ♪

75 SIXTH SENSE

All answers have six letters. 1 to 6 start in the outer circle and are written towards the centre. 7 to 12 go round the rings in a clockwise direction.

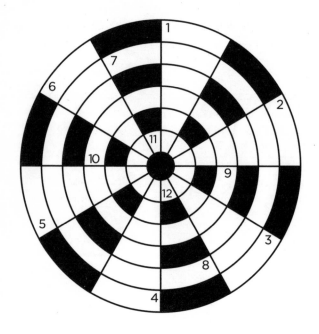

MODERATE PUZZLES

Questions

1   What is the second of Vivaldi's *Four Seasons*?
2   What was the nationality of composer Hector Berlioz?
3   What name is given to a number of series of songs on a single theme?
4   Which Italian was the first major name to be heard on a gramophone?
5   What is the combination of voices at the same pitch called?
6   What name is shared by the voice of a songbird and part of the neck a singer must take great care of?
7   What is the first name of American pianist Perahia?
8   Which term means to introduce a newcomer to their chosen career?
9   What is another name for long-playing vinyl records?
10 Which opera star Jessye was said to have a voice like a 'grand mansion of sound'?
11 Which German composer's choral works included the *German Requiem*?
12 Which brass instrument resembles a smaller, shorter trumpet?

76 **HONEYCOMB**

All answers have six letters. They fit into the grid in either a clockwise or anti-clockwise direction. The first letter of the answer to Clue 1 (S) and the direction in which the word is written have been given. After that you'll have to work out in which hexagonal cell the answer begins, and in which direction it goes.

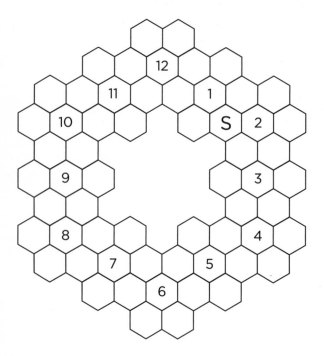

Clues

1   Time of a season name checked in *Porgy and Bess* (clockwise)
2   There were 11 of these musicians performing in the *Twelve Days of Christmas*
3   Polish-born composer who wrote almost exclusively for the piano
4   Refers to music that is sung
5   American composer famous for movies including *Titanic* and *Apollo 13*
6   The parts of a song that precede a chorus or refrain
7   The 'John Dunbar Theme' is from the movie *Dances with* _____
8   Paganini was a virtuoso on this instrument
9   Alto versions of 8
10   Composer William who wrote the opera *Troilus and Cressida*
11   Musical term meaning fast
12   German composer who accepted his Oscar for *Dune* wearing a bathrobe

77 FIND HER

Solve the quickfire clues below to find answers that all contain the word 'her'. It might appear at the beginning of the word, in the middle or at the end. If the answer includes several words, only one contains 'her'.

1   Three-act opera by Bizet (3,5,7)
2   Comic opera by Benjamin Britten, premiered in 1947 (6,7)
3   Originally an Alpine folk instrument with five melody strings
4   Austrian conductor, who was artistic director of the Salzburg Festival from 1956–60 (7,3,7)
5   Musical term, the Italian for 'joke'
6   American composer and conductor who wrote the music for *Psycho* and *Citizen Kane*

78 TO THE POINT

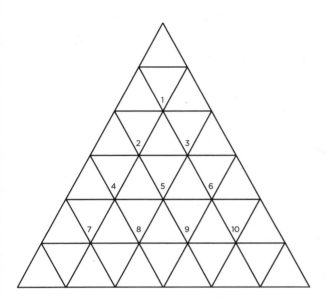

Each answer contains four letters. The first letter goes in a numbered triangle, the second letter directly above it, the third letter to the right and the fourth to the left.

Clues

1 First name of Welsh composer Jenkins
2 A music one is a web page updated frequently with the latest music news
3 A group of three musicians
4 They follow the Good and the Bad in a movie famous for its soundtrack
5 First name of the playwright, actor and singer after whom London's Albery Theatre was renamed
6 Describes music performed as you listen rather than recorded
7 A religious song
8 Dance from the *Nutcracker Suite*, the *Sugar _____ Fairy*
9 The siku is an Andean panpipe from this South American country
10 In Handel's *Hallelujah Chorus*, the words 'Forever and _____' are repeated

79 **TAKE FIVE**

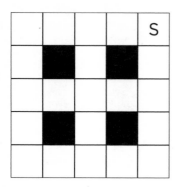

Solve the musical clues, which are listed at random. All the answers contain five letters. Fit the answers in the grid, going either across or down. There is a starter letter to help you on the way. There is only one way to fit all the words in the grid.

Clues

Male rulers in the title of a Debbie Wiseman work

The Sorcerer's Apprentice composer

Discernment and appreciation of quality in the arts

Minimalist American composer, _____ Reich

First performance

Ronald _____, composer of *Sailing By*

80 FILLERS

In each group, find a single music-linked word to fill the spaces and complete the longer words.

1 R E _ _ _ _ S E
    S _ _ _ _ S
    _ _ _ _ S A Y

2 S T _ _ _ S
    F L _ _ _
    F _ _ _ W A Y

3 F _ _ _ _
    G _ _ _ _ N
    D I _ _ _ _ D

81 COMPOSE YOURSELF

1						
2	I					
3						
4						
5			E			
6						
7						

You need to stay calm and composed for this puzzle!

Place all the seven-letter music-linked words below in the grid in the right order to reveal the name of a composer who lived through most of last century. The two vowels in his surname are already in place.

ANDANTE
CORNETS
QUARTET
REPRISE
TAVENER
VESPERS
WISEMAN

82 **BAX WORDS**

The name of a composer is hidden in the sentences below, but it has been written backwards. Look for a continuous line of letters from right to left to spell out a composer's surname. Arnold Bax isn't to be found!

1   They headed south towards Peru after their sell-out performances in the USA.
2   For the final piece in the concert, extra players took to the stage to augment the orchestra.
3   There are some names I wish I hadn't called the over-loud tenors in the second row.
4   In that famous piece *Nimrod* I wonder at the beauty of the orchestration.

83 **MOVIE A TO Z**

Here are the names of some movies with music that has featured in the Classic FM Hall of Fame. The letters are shown in alphabetical order. Rearrange them to find the movie titles.

1   A A D E E F H I K L O O R R R S S T T   (five words)

2   A C E E E E F G H I I M N N N S T T V   (three words)

3   D E E F G H H I L N O O R R S T T   (five words)

4   C E E H H K L L M O O R S S   (two words)

84 MY MISTAKE

Chaos and confusion reign in the publicity office, which has resulted in errors on the posters advertising the film club's new programme. It's only one wrong letter, but it creates a new word and gives the film title a whole new meaning! From the clues, work out the incorrect titles and what they should really be.

Clues

1   Hirsute worker in clay   (two words)
2   Sausage past its sell-by date   (two words)
3   Archaeological find in the American Midwest   (two words)

85 **REARRANGEMENT**

There are two clues to help you find two solutions. The first clue leads you to a general word. The second clue leads you to the name of a composer. You will need all your skills as an arranger, as the second word is an anagram of the first – it has all the same letters, but in a different order.

1   Legendary Australian tennis player Rod
French composer, famous for his *Bolero* favoured by ice dancers Torvill and Dean

2   Close by
Composer of the anthem *Rule Britannia*

3   Slow-moving creature, a byword for laziness
He set *The Planets* to music!

4   Marsh bird of the heron family
Born in Lowestoft, he wrote *Peter Grimes*, and was awarded a life peerage in 1976

5   Former US President Reagan
Trumpeter and composer Malcolm who wrote the music for *The Bridge on the River Kwai*

86 LUCKY NUMBERS

Test your musical knowledge and your basic arithmetic skills in one puzzle.

1   What do you get if you multiply the number of Beethoven's *Choral Symphony*, by the number of *Years in Tibet* in the movie classic?

2   What do you get if you take away the number of operas Beethoven wrote from the number of *Last Songs* by Richard Strauss?

3   What do you get if you add up the digits in Tchaikovsky's masterpiece commemorating the expulsion of Napoleonic troops from Moscow?

4   What do you get if you add the number of the disastrous Apollo mission, whose film soundtrack was created by James Horner, and the number of seconds suggested in the Minute waltz by Chopin?

87 **MUSIC BOX**

A	L	T	O	M	T
X	L	R	D	J	U
Q	B	O	R	E	N
A	B	C	U	S	E
A	U	S	E	D	Z
P	O	D	E	S	F

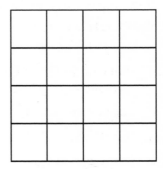

In a word square, the same words can be read both across and down. Your challenge is to create a musical word square in the empty grid using the four music-related words hidden in the letter box. The words in the letter box all appear in straight lines that can go in any direction. They all contain four letters.

88 FORWARD PLANNING

There are two clues to help you find two solutions. The first clue leads you to a general word. The second clue leads you to a music-based word. The solutions are very similar, but in the second word the middle letter has moved *forwards* in the alphabet.

1 Consecrate, sanctify
   Composer Sir Arthur

2 Senior person
   The Bernstein famous for the soundtrack of *Ghostbusters*

3 Unlock, or remove a restriction from a gate
   Jay, who wrote *The Ashokan Farewell*

4 Divide, apportion
   Composer of the music for *The Silence of the Lambs*

89 IN MY LIFETIME

Look at these important events. What year did they take place?
Decide which of the three performers listed was alive at the time.

1 The year the first Academy Awards ceremony took place.
In whose lifetime did this event take place?
a)   Aaron Copland
b)   Philip Glass
c)   Leos Janáček

2 The year that Classic FM was founded.
In whose lifetime did this event take place?
a)   Samuel Barber
b)   Leonard Bernstein
c)   Harrison Birtwistle

3 The year Queen Elizabeth II celebrated her Silver Jubilee.
In whose lifetime did this event take place?
a)   Alison Balsom
b)   Benjamin Britten
c)   Lesley Garrett

90 **MAJOR SEVENTH**

The classical music-related words below all contain seven letters. Put them in the grid either across or down. There is only one way to fit all the words in. One letter has been given to start you off.

BRITTEN
CLASSIC
CORNETS
ENCORES
GORECKI
HAITINK
RECITAL
REQUIEM
REWRITE
PRELUDE
UKELELE
VIVALDI

91 **WISE WORDS**

Your challenge is to work out part of a quotation by a musician describing how to improve your playing.

Solve the clues and put the eight-letter answers horizontally in the first grid. Reading downwards, column A will reveal the name of the musician.

Use the first grid to help you complete the second one by putting in the letters that correspond to the grid coordinates. The completed second grid will reveal the rest of the quotation, which begins 'Focus on those one or two notes and get that ringing quality and …'.

	A	B	C	D	E	F	G	H
1								
2								
3								
4								
5								
6								
7								
8								
9								

MODERATE PUZZLES

Clues

1 Instrument with the lowest pitch in part of the percussion section (4,4)
2 In Tchaikovsky's famous *Overture* the first two digits make this number
3 Reference to the USA in Dvorak's Symphony No. 9 (3,5)
4 The interval between two parts of a play or opera
5 The fifth note of the diatonic scale of any key, or most influential
6 Stress laid on notes or phrases to give a special effect
7 Brass instrument with a slide
8 Three-cornered instrument
9 Pick out one instrument as separate from another

H9	E3	G1	D4			H7	F5	B8	H6		C3	B2	G8	G3	
F6	A7	B1	F3	H5		E9	C7								
B9	H8	B6	E4	H2	A5		H1	B5	B7	F2					
F7	G9		G4	D6	G2		C1	D8	C5	B3					

92 ON GOOD TERMS

```
O D N E C S E R C Z H O Q U R
T R L N A G Y T G L Z T U S E
M S C A L E E L P P E R A B P
Y I W H B N A A R I M T V I E
S H N J E R C E A Z O N E E T
L T Y I U S S G H Z O R R P I
A I A T M T T S I M U R T T
T L A C O X E R T C T B E T I
N N A P C H E I A A L M V T O
E I N R C A S O N T P Y A P N
D O G T G O T G T O I L T L H
I A O C P O I O N S F O S W Y
C R U M B S M O R R E A N U D
C A O T A G E L T I Z R O I E
A C R P S N O I S S E R P X E
```

The names of various musical terms are hidden in the word square. All words are in straight lines that run horizontally, vertically or diagonally. They may read forwards or backwards. One word appears twice – what is it?

ACCIDENTAL	LARGO	PRESTO	STACCATO
COMPOSITION	LEGATO	QUAVER	STAVE
CRESCENDO	MINIM	REPETITION	TEMPO
CROTCHET	NATURAL	SCALE	
EXPRESSION	ORCHESTRATION	SHARP	
FLAT	PIZZICATO	SIGNATURE	

93 **SILENT VOICES**

The four voices that make up the four-part harmony in these vocal works have been replaced by question marks. Each question mark could be an S (soprano), A (alto), T (tenor) or B (bass). Work out the missing letters to identify the vocal works.

1   F ? U ? ? (Gounod)

2   M ? C ? E ? H (Verdi)

3   ? ? N N H ? U ? E R (Wagner)

4   R U ? ? L K ? (Dvorak)

5   ? U R ? N D O ? (Puccini)

94 **SHAPE UP**

In this puzzle, the letters in the names of famous composers have been replaced by symbols.

RAVEL is

Who are the other famous names?

1

95 LIKES

An up-and-coming young classical violinist named Ivor Bow has created a new social media profile. He put a lot of work into it, and was hoping for an instant rush of visitors and 'likes'. However, after five days online he has seen just a steady rise in the total number of likes he has received.

Since the end of the first day, he has received 60 additional likes each day. At the end of day five, Ivor has registered 1,000 likes.

How many people had responded at the end of the first day?

96 INNER CALM

Solve the clues. Starting in the top left-hand square of the grid, write the answers moving inwards in a clockwise direction. The words overlap with *at least* the last letter of one answer becoming the first letter of the next answer. Calmly does it!

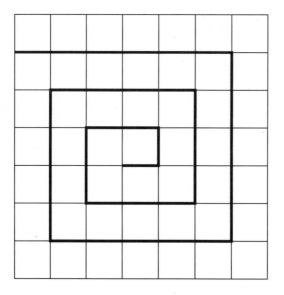

MODERATE PUZZLES

Clues

1 Saxophonist Jess
2 Gershwin-scored film, *An _____ in Paris*
3 Term meaning 'at a walking pace'
4 Welsh baritone Bryn
5 Opera star Lott, now a dame
6 Sing, as in the alpine mountains
7 She shares an opera title with Samson
8 Bernard, Dutch conductor of many international orchestras
9 Austrian-American Erich who won Oscars in the heyday of Hollywood
10 Aria from *Madame Butterfly*, *One Fine _____*

97 CODA

20	■	19	■	23	3	10	2	1	4	2	26	7
1 T	2 R	3 U	4 E	■	1	■	10	■	10	■	7	■
20	■	21	■	1	10	24	4	6	1	2	7	■
9	17	1	20	8	4	■	24	■	7	■	4	■
4	■	10	■	■	2	■	17	■	■	26	■	24
2	4	24	26	7	■	24	2	4	13	20	4	2
10	■	17	■	■	6	10	1	■	■	13	■	17
2	4	6	24	17	9	15	■	6	24	4	10	25
7	■	4	■	■	3	■	17	■	■	26	■	17
■	11	■	14	■	11	■	16	4	26	20	4	18
10	2	24	4	11	11	20	17	■	■	11	■	20
■	20	■	10	■	26	■	4	■	6	5	17	4
4	15	4	26	22	4	20	6	6	■	1	■	12

MODERATE PUZZLES

Each letter of the alphabet has been replaced by a number. Work out which number represents which letter to complete the crossword-style grid. Words can go across or down. One word has been given to start you off.

HINTS:
The letters in the word down the right-hand column spell out a famous composer.
When you have cracked the code, the letters 1.5.4./26.17.12.4/18.17.2/1. 5.2.4.4/17.2.10.9.11.4.6. spell out an opera by this composer.

Fill in the grid below with the letters corresponding to each number as you discover them.

1	2	3	4	5	6	7	8	9	10	11	12	13
14	15	16	17	18	19	20	21	22	23	24	25	26

98 ADDERS

Each conundrum leads to a music-related word.

1   What do you get if you add a mobile-device download to praise?
2   Who do you get if you add a set of dealt cards to the Spanish for the?
3   What do you get if you add an abbreviated higher learning establishment to a male offspring?
4   Who do you get if you add an American policeman to a successful aircraft touchdown?
5   What do you get if you add the official in charge of a soccer match to precipitation?

99 **TRANSPOSING**

Transposing changes the pitches in a musical work without altering the relationship between the notes. Our arranger has applied the same idea to the lyrics!

Each letter of the alphabet has changed position and the change is consistent for every letter, so if A was transposed to B, B would become C, C would become D, and so on.

Here are the words of a popular carol after the letters have been transposed. The arranger has kept the transposition using musical notes, so A could be a B, C, D, E, F or G. Work out the transposition rule to read the lyrics.

HINTS: Shorter words can provide a clue as there are less options that they could be. Also, look for letters that appear together and at the frequency of individual letters.

SRGI / MR / VSCEP / HEZMH'W / GMXC,
WXSSH / E / PSAPC / GEXXPI / WLIH,
ALIVI / E / QSXLIV / PEMH / LIV / FEFC
MR / E / QERKIV / JSV / LMW / FIH.

100 **CRYPTIC**

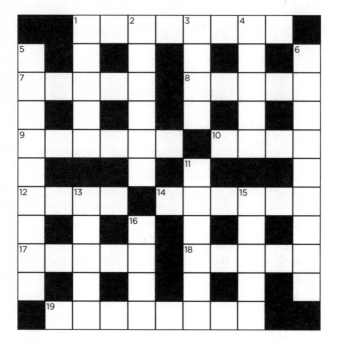

MODERATE PUZZLES

A cryptic crossword to massage the mind.

Across

1 Butchers chopped up unfinished work by genius (8)

7 Lab I'd destroyed as I improvise (2,3)

8 Anger gives way to vocal limits (5)

9 Stream innovative head of music (6)

10 Point dropped in Rhone and revised by instrument (4)

12 Cat's lives equate to Beethoven symphonies (4)

14 Cut led somehow to sweet and soft sound (6)

17 Poet Lorca found rewritten as part of Elgar's *Sea Pictures* (5)

18 Diver brings up Italian composer (5)

19 Part also found in romantic rural symphony (8)

Down

1 Oslo's players perform alone (5)

2 The brewers appeared to be slaves of *Nabucco* (6)

3 A feathered friend we hear, but with religious songs (4)

4 No rod needed in this final movement (5)

5 A choir man retunes a mouth organ (9)

6 Bert's nine variations from this American composer (9)

11 Wobble note (6)

13 Roman version of Bellini opera (5)

15 Christmas song from this lady (5)

16 Apartment of note (4)

CHALLENGING
PUZZLES

101 **KEY-BOARD**

	G	C		mj			mn	
		B	A					
					F		mj	
		mj		D			E	
D				C			B	
	B			A		mn	C	
C								G
		E			F		mj	
B	F		D					mn

In this puzzle, each block of nine squares must contain the letters of the keys A, B, C, D, E, F and G, along with mj to denote a major key and mn to denote a minor key. Every row (going across) and every column (going down) must contain nine different keys.

102 **MINDFULNESS**

To solve this puzzle you need to use what you cannot see. Focus your mind on the letters of the alphabet that do NOT appear in the box. All the missing letters can be used once, and three of them can be used twice to form the name of a composer.

103 **EASE INTO EIGHT**

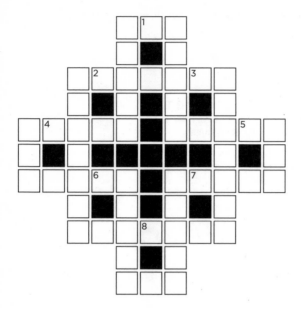

Solve the eight clues to find the eight-letter answers. The first letter of the answer goes in the numbered square in the grid, and the answer can go clockwise or anti-clockwise. You must work out which direction it goes.

Clues

1   Italian violinist and composer who died in Nice in 1840
2   Scandinavian great-grandfather of fellow composer Lauri Porra, husband of conductor Dalia Stasevska
3   Two-act opera by Peter Maxwell Davies
4   Composer whose greatest success was *Cavalleria Rusticana*
5   String instrument used by Verdi for atmosphere in *Otello* and *Falstaff*
6   Fifth section in the sung mass or as part of a requiem (5,3)
7   17th-century-born composer whose oboe concerto was the first by an Italian to be published
8   The crumhorn is an early example of this group of instruments

104 IN THE SHADE

Take a break in the shade with this puzzle and work out what composer Gustav Mahler said about his Symphony No 1.

Solve the clues and put the answers horizontally in the upper grid. All answers have eight letters, except line 6. Take the letters in the shaded squares from each answer and place them vertically in the lower grid to reveal the Mahler quotation.

Clues

1   Musical setting for a religious text such as Handel's *Messiah*
2   He wrote over 600 songs; two of his symphonies were *Tragic* and *Unfinished*
3   A shorter work than a symphony such as Britten's *da Requiem*
4   1964 movie music by Ron Grainger, 633 _____?
5   1882 Gilbert and Sullivan operetta set in Parliament
6   The fifth note of a major scale (3) / Herrmann and Morricone have great success with music for this branch of the arts (4)
7   Another word for peaceful and calm, not just in music
8   French songs
9   Italian-born keyboard player and piano manufacturer, who died in England in 1832
10 Repetition of a melody at a higher or lower pitch

105 **LENTO**

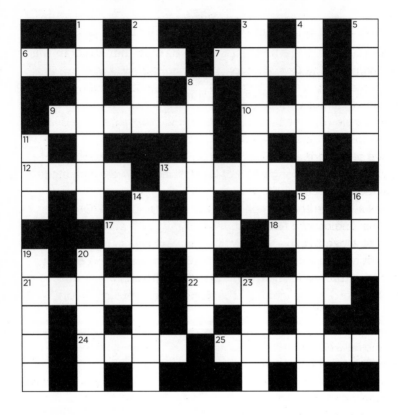

CHALLENGING PUZZLES

A no-tricks crossword.

Across

6 *Cuculus canorus* heard by Delius (6)
7 First name of *The Dam Busters* film score composer (4)
9 Instrumental music for soloist or ensemble (6)
10 City whose conservatoire was named after Verdi in 1901 (5)
12 Singing promoted by the Anacreontic Society (4)
13 One of seven written by Brahms; one of a number in Latin by Mozart (5)
17 Highest digit in a number title of an overture by Tchaikovsky (5)
18 First word of a 1689 opera by Purcell (4)
21 Composer who revived the fortunes of Viennese operetta in the early 20th century (5)
22 US opera singer Jessye who established her School of the Arts in Georgia (6)
24 Tone muffler (4)
25 *Ride* by creator of 6 Across (6)

Down

1 Shostakovich symphony dedicated to this month (7)
2 Spanish dance (4)
3 Instrument played by Alison Balsom (7)
4 It may be pentatonic, diatonic or whole tone (5)
5 Psalm or canticle (5)
8 Instrument introduced to the USA by Sousa (9)
11 Era, such as jazz (3)
14 Fluctuation of pitch of a single note (7)
15 Queen in works by Britten, Mendelssohn and Purcell (7)
16 Haydn Symphony to play with (3)
19 Master of the Queen's music in Elizabeth II's coronation year (5)
20 Part of the percussion section (5)
23 First word of Arne's most famous chorus (4)

106 **CHILL OUT**

The letters that appear in the word CHILL have been removed from the names of various composers. Replace the letters and complete the names.

1 P U _ _ _ N _

2 _ _ E R U B _ N _

3 B O _ _ _ E R _ N _

4 P O N _ _ _ E _ _ _

5 _ O _ A T E _ _ _

6 D A _ _ A P _ _ _ O _ A

Which THREE composers have the same first name, and what is it?

107 **PASSCODE**

Entrance to the Fakehem manuscript library is controlled by a number passcode that has to be input on the keypad by the main door. The passcode is made up of the numbers 1 to 7, with each number used once. The difference between adjacent digits is always greater than one. The final digit is half the value of the penultimate digit. No two odd numbers are ever adjacent to each other.

What is the passcode number?

108 FAR, FAR AWAY

```
N  I  A  S  E  D  I  R  B  E  H  F
X  E  W  L  O  N  D  O  N  K  T  I
E  P  W  Y  P  A  R  I  S  I  D  N
D  O  H  W  Q  I  N  O  N  Z  U  G
N  L  S  P  O  A  N  T  F  N  L  A
A  I  I  U  I  R  A  E  I  Y  H  L
R  S  N  L  P  G  L  A  L  R  C  S
G  H  A  D  E  R  T  D  I  U  T  C
O  T  P  L  A  N  N  A  E  C  O  A
I  B  S  J  U  P  I  T  E  R  C  V
R  U  G  O  X  F  O  R  D  E  S  E
A  D  M  C  I  D  R  O  N  M  R  O
```

Faraway places have often provided inspiration for composers. All the faraway words in the grid are linked to musical pieces. They all appear in straight lines that can go horizontally, vertically or diagonally. They may read forwards or backwards.

When you have found all the words, rearrange the *unused* letters in row 12 and column 9 to discover a part of the world where a composer made his home for a number of years.

ALPINE
FINGAL'S CAVE
HEBRIDES
ITALIAN
JUPITER
LONDON
MERCURY
MOUNTAIN
NEW WORLD
NORDIC
OCEAN
OXFORD
PARIS
POLISH
RIO GRANDE
SCOTCH
SPANISH
TINTAGEL

109 **LET GO**

Look at the words below. Follow the instructions to let go of some of the words to reveal the title of a piece of 20th-century music.

	A	B	C	D
1	Bizet	Judith	Britten	Purcell
2	Rossini	Arnold	Orff	Verdi
3	Menuhin	Job	Messiaen	Elgar
4	Delius	Elijah	Rutter	Wagner
5	Borodin	Joseph	Grappelli	Benedetti
6	Samson	Upside	Walton	Paganini
7	Bax	Down	Ravel	Gounod
8	Mozart	Violin	Jenkins	Byrd

1 Let go of composers in column C who were born in the 20th century.
2 Let go of any composer in row 7 whose name ends with a Roman numeral.
3 Let go of any composer in column A whose first name is longer than his second.
4 In row 2, let go of any composers who lived until they were over 80.
5 In column D, let go of any composers whose first names were shared by English kings.
6 Let go of the names of any oratorios.
7 Let go of any violinists.

110 **SING ALONG**

A new choir called The Logical Singers has organised a six-week schedule of rehearsals to see if there is enough interest for the group to get established. The first meeting has an encouraging turnout of 28 singers (although the offer of free wine might be something to do with this). Numbers drop to 11 for the second rehearsal. They continue to fall, with six singers attending the third rehearsal and only three people turning up for the fourth. The fifth rehearsal is slightly better and five people attend. The organiser decides that she will only carry on if the number attending the final rehearsal improves.

What happens to The Logical Singers?

111 MISSING FROM THE MOVIES

The vowels in these movie titles have been removed. Put them back to reveal the names of movies that have some of the best film scores of all time.

1 G L D T R

2 T H L S T S M R (three words)

3 N T R S T L L R

4 N T M T D (four words)

5 N G L S N D D M N S (three words)

They are all written by the same composer. Who is he?

112 STAR GAZING

Seven stars of the music world (composers and singers) have had the letters in their surnames rearranged in alphabetical order. Work out the names, then fit them vertically in the grid so that the shaded diagonal squares spell out the name of a famous opera. The list is not in the correct order.

CLUE: The first letter in column 1 begins with a letter in the first half of the alphabet.

1	2	3	4	5	6	7

Placido	D G I M N O O
John	A E E N R T V
Michael	E I P P T T T
Kathleen	E E F I R R R
Andrés	A E G I O S V
Montserrat	A A B C E L L
Joaquin	D G I O O R R

113 **NUMBER NAMES**

Each letter has been given a numerical value from 1 to 8. The total value of each word is reached by adding up the individual letters. No two letters have the same number.

A R I A S = 11

M A S S = 16

C A L L S = 26

M A R I A C A L L A S = 41

L A S C A L A M I L A N = 53

We all know that CLASSIC FM is beyond price, but what is the value of the word C L A S S I C?

114 **CLOUD NINE**

Each number from 1 to 9 represents a different letter of the alphabet. Solve the clues and write the letters in the appropriate spaces in the grid to reveal a word with a musical link.

1	2	3	4	5	6	7	8	9

Clues

a) Symphony originally attributed to Haydn   8 5 2

b) Emphasis on a note or chord   7 4 4 9 3 8

c) Holes on a wind instrument   1 8 5 6 1

115 BEHIND THE SCENES

Which composers are hiding behind the scenes in the sentences below? Discover them by joining words or parts of words together.

1   I like to hear new, innovative music when I can.
2   The songs and rhythms of Africa generally receive a warm reception here.
3   As you know, I do rewrite phrases from time to time if they are too difficult.
4   That this newcomer is a genius is my theory for certain.

116 **HAVE A BREAK**

The letters in the names of two different pieces of music have been split and rearranged into a line. The letters remain in the correct order for each word. In each case, both words have the same number of letters. Can you work out what the pieces of music are?

1 F N A I D B E L U I C O C O

2 G L T O R U R A N I A D O N T A

3 F A P L A S R S T I F A F F A L

117 WHAT AM I?

My first is in RHYTHM
But isn't in RHYME.
My second's in THEME
But isn't in TIME.
My third is in OPERA
And also in DANCE.
My fourth is in DREAMLIKE
And also in TRANCE.
My fifth is in ACTOR
And also in STAGE.
My sixth is in PAPER
But isn't in PAGE.
My seventh's in VIEW
And also in SEE.
I hope very soon that
You may visit me.

118 BLOWING BUBBLES

There are three bubbles and the names of three pieces of music to be formed. The question mark stands for a mystery letter, which appears in all three titles. Use all the letters in each bubble once, including the mystery letter, to find the names of the pieces, which are all the works of a British composer.

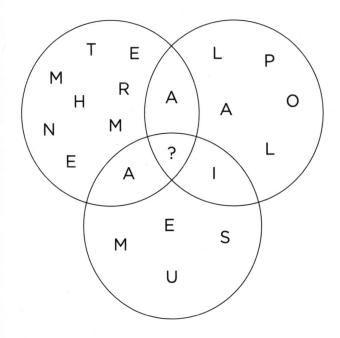

119 **HALF FULL?**

Is your glass half full or half empty? The following puzzle calls for positive thinking.

The clues below are listed at random, but they each have a four-letter answer. Solve the clues, then write the words in the grid so that the last two letters of one answer become the first two letters of the next. Each first letter appears in a numbered space.

1		2		3		4		5			

Clues

The first word in the title of a Swiss painting from which Rachmaninoff created a symphonic poem

The last part of a piece or melody

The first name of Spanish flamenco guitarist and composer of *Ojos Azules*

King who is the subject of an opera by Aribert Reimann

Low platform from which the conductor might conduct

120 **RING CYCLE**

Solve the clues, which are in no particular order, and slot the seven-letter answers into their correct places in the ring. The last letter of one answer forms the first letter of the next. Answer 1 begins with a letter S.

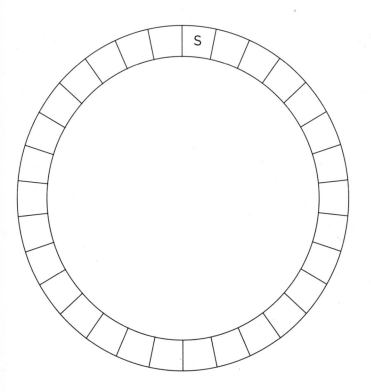

Clues
Drums
Mendelssohn's Symphony No. 4
US composer Max, who became a percussionist before working on electronic music
Light, playful piece, the Italian for 'joke' or 'jest'
Rhythm that emphasises the weak stroke in a bar

121 **COMMITTEE MEETING**

The Great Ditherington Music Festival held a committee meeting. Five members sat at a round table. Read the minutes of the meeting, then work out where each of the five people – Julie, Dave, Carol, Andrea and Phil – was sitting and what their role was.

7.30 pm Meeting called to order by the Chair.

7.31 pm Julie gives apologies for the Treasurer.

7.32 pm The Treasurer appears, takes a seat between the two gentlemen and apologises for being late. Julie apologises for making the earlier apology.

7.35 pm The Treasurer, although asked to be brief by the Chair, proceeds with a 25-minute presentation, including a slideshow that doesn't work properly.

8.00 pm Dave suggests that the Artistic Director postpones his plans for discussing ideas for the Music Festival until all funding has been formally approved. The Artistic Director and Chair agree. Carol and the Social Secretary disagree.

8.05 pm The lady sitting directly to the left of Phil complains that she is being undervalued and threatens to walk out. The Membership Secretary gets up to open the door. The lady storms out as the Membership Secretary returns to his seat between the two remaining ladies.

8.07 pm Andrea decides to officially suspend the meeting.

122 TOKEN GESTURE

An outdoor classical music festival is going to feature various acts and events over a weekend. Tokens are issued to festival-goers, which can be used to gain entry to the various performances. Performances are arranged into three price bands. Band A events require one token to gain admittance. Band B events require three tokens, while Band C events require four tokens.

One festival-goer manages to see 12 different performances, including at least one concert in Band A, Band B and Band C. She uses a total of 24 tokens during the weekend.

How many Band A events did she watch?

123 PERFECT FIFTH

Solve the clues, which are listed at random. Each answer contains five letters. Complete the grid so that each answer starts in a space with an odd number and ends in the space with the even number that is one greater. To give you a perfect start, the letter in space 1 is P.

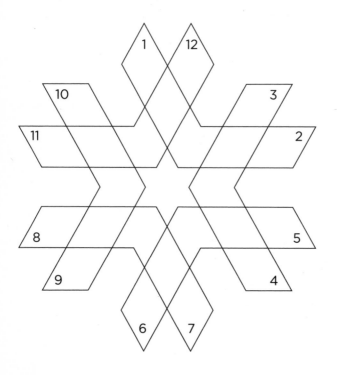

Clues
Voices a lost medley
Sounds wicked but created inexpensive opera
Ward off attack with English composer
Track behind a film
Move a rung to reveal folk songwriter
Dream about Jenkins' Man

124 TAKE NOTE

Each letter that appears in the treble clef (A, B, C, D, E, F and G) has been replaced by a musical note. The other letters of the alphabet are in place. Work out the words then match them up to find the surname of a composer and one of their compositions in each case. There is a symphony, a cantata and a rhapsody.

♪ ♪ ♪ R

♪ ♪ L I U S

♪ ♪ ♪ L ♪ I ♪ ♪

H ♪ Y ♪ N

♪ R I ♪ ♪   ♪ ♪ I R

♪ ♪ ♪ T H O V ♪ N

125 **SIXTH SENSE**

All answers have six letters. 1 to 6 start in the outer circle and are written towards the centre. 7 to 12 go round the rings in a clockwise direction.

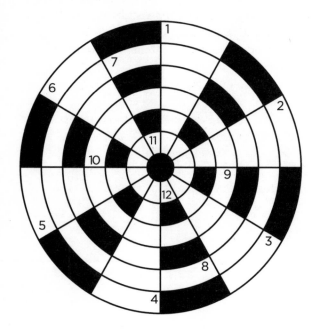

CHALLENGING PUZZLES

Questions

1 Who wrote *The Flying Dutchman* and *Das Rheingold*?
2 Who takes the title role in the Gilbert and Sullivan opera with Ko-Ko and Yum-Yum?
3 Hark! Which angels sing in the title of a popular carol?
4 What is the anglicised first name of the composer in Clue 5?
5 Who wrote *Water Music* and *Judas Maccabaeus*?
6 What is the first name of British opera singer Miss Alder?
7 What might describe the occupation of Lieutenant Pinkerton in Puccini's *Madame Butterfly*?
8 Which term means that music must be played smoothly?
9 What is the capital city of José Carreras' home country?
10 Which city numbered Mozart and Beethoven among its residents?
11 Who wrote the *Peterloo Overture*, commissioned by the TUC to commemorate the massacre in Manchester in 1819?
12 What was the first name of the Australian opera star who had a peach dessert named after her?

126 **HONEYCOMB**

All answers have six letters. They fit into the grid in either a clockwise or anti-clockwise direction. The first letter of the answer to Clue 1 (G) and the direction in which the word is written have been given. After that you'll have to work out in which hexagonal cell the answer begins, and in which direction it goes.

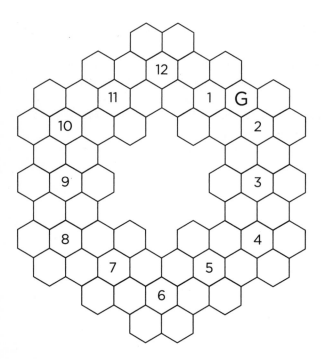

CHALLENGING PUZZLES

Clues

1   First name of the British composer who wrote *Dies Natalis* (anti-clockwise)
2   English composer who wrote *The Sea* in 1911 and was Benjamin Britten's teacher
3   First name adopted by the composer who was born Israel Baline
4   Roberto Alagna is this type of performer
5   First name of Romanian soprano Georgiou
6   Continent in the name of a 1980s film whose theme won an Academy Award for Best Original Score
7   Country in which Bradford composer Delius died
8   Opera in four acts by Bizet
9   Subject of an opera by Rimsky-Korsakov, _____ *and Salieri*
10   First name of the composer granted a licence by Elizabeth I to print and publish music
11   Handel's *Water Music* was said to have been composed for a royal water party on this river
12   French composer whose first opera was *Hippolyte et Aricie*, performed after his 50th birthday

127 TIN MINING

Solve the quickfire clues below. Each answer contains the word 'tin'. It might appear at the beginning of the word, in the middle or at the end. If the answer includes several words, only one contains 'tin'.

1   Instrument with hexagonal casings connected by bellows

2   Czech composer whose operas include *The Miracles of Mary* and *Comedy on the Bridge*

3   Tone poem by Sir Arnold Bax written the year after the Great War

4   German-born composer (1741–1816) who wrote the 'vocal romance' known today as *Plaisir D'Amour*

5   Part of the City of London, on the soundtrack of *Wolf Hall*, written by Debbie Wiseman (6,6)

6   1970 piece by Stanley Myers, popularised as the theme from *The Deer Hunter*

128 TO THE POINT

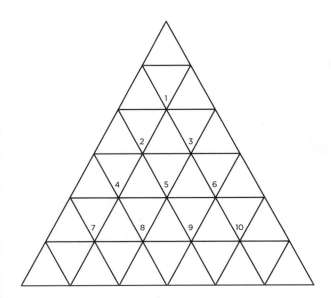

Each answer contains four letters. The first letter goes in a numbered triangle, the second letter directly above it, the third letter to the right and the fourth to the left.

Clues

1 Saint-Saens' opera *La Belle Hélène* is about Helen of _____
2 London park where open-air music from the Proms is performed
3 *F* means this in musical notation
4 To indicate a tempo or rhythm by waving a baton or tapping
5 An original musical thought
6 Opera by Bartók, _____ *Bluebeard's Castle*
7 River that Orpheus enchanted Charon to carry the souls of the dead across in *Orpheus in the Underworld*
8 Aled Jones song, *Did You Not Hear My* _____
9 Used in clarinets, saxophones, oboes and bassoons
10 A song begins 'Speed bonnie boat like a bird on the wing' and ends 'Over the sea to _____'

129 **TAKE FIVE**

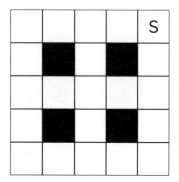

Solve the musical clues, which are listed at random. All the answers contain five letters. Fit the answers in the grid, going either across or down. There is a starter letter to help you on the way. There is only one way to fit all the words in the grid.

Clues

Composer whose last opera was *Falstaff*

And did his hands in ancient times, write this stirring anthem?

One of Major Stanley's daughter in *Pirates*, but not Mabel

This name features with *Lazarus* in a Vaughan Williams work

Cellist Jacqueline who famously played Elgar's Concerto (2,3)

Dame Ethel, composer of *The Wreckers*

130 **FILLERS**

In each group, find a single music-linked word to fill the spaces and complete the longer words.

1   T H _ _ _ _
     B _ _ _ _
     D _ _ _ _ E D

2   C _ _ _ _
     _ _ _ _ O R E
     A R _ _ _ _ I N G

3   _ _ _ _ O O N
     S _ _ _ _ E N
     _ _ _ _ Y

131 **COMPOSE YOURSELF**

1						
2						
3						
4						
5						
6						
7						

You need to stay calm and composed for this puzzle!

Place all the seven-letter music-linked words below in the grid in the right order to reveal the name of a composer involved in one of the most famous rivalries of all time.

BALLADS
JANACEK
KOSHIRO
POULENC
RECITAL
SMETANA
VIVALDI

132 **BAX WORDS**

The name of a composer is hidden in the sentences below, but it has been written backwards. Look for a continuous line of letters from right to left to spell out a composer's surname. Arnold Bax isn't to be found!

1   Having entered the music competition, the win is so rewarding.
2   After a tetchy morning rehearsal, a light lunch curbed the grumbles of the orchestra.
3   In *The Mikado*, Nanki-Poo is a wandering minstrel hammering out his songs in the street.
4   It was a dirge llamas would have been ashamed of!

133 **MOVIE A TO Z**

Here are the names of some movies with music that has featured in the Classic FM Hall of Fame. The letters are shown in alphabetical order. Rearrange them to find the movie titles.

1 AAAACEIIIMNNNPRRS (four words)

2 ABCDGIIIKKLLMNOORT (four words)

3 ACCEEEEEHIJMNORRRSSSSTTVY (five words)

4 ADEGHHIKKNRTT (three words)

134 MY MISTAKE

Chaos and confusion reign in the publicity office, which has resulted in errors on the posters advertising the film club's new programme. It's only one wrong letter, but it creates a new word and gives the film title a whole new meaning! From the clues, work out the incorrect titles and what they should really be.

Clues

1   Referee retaliates after receiving criticism at the cricket match (four words)
2   The potholing adventures of a lowly military man   (three words)
3   Friendly meetings with Richard III   (six words)

135 **REARRANGEMENT**

There are two clues to help you find two solutions. The first clue leads you to a general word. The second clue leads you to the name of a composer. You will need all your skills as an arranger, as the second word is an anagram of the first – it has all the same letters, but in a different order.

1   District of New York, noted for its jazz bands in the 1920s
    Bohemian-Austrian well-known for opera

2   Meat merchants
    Trout not meat was the product of this composer

3   A coal miner
    Violinist who became chamber musician to Queen Christina of Sweden

4   Greek wine infused with resin
    English organist whose oratorio *The Crucifixion* is one of his best-known works

5   When referring to animals this word means domesticated, not at all wild
    French composer of *Manon* and *Werther*

136 **LUCKY NUMBERS**

Test your musical knowledge and your basic arithmetic skills in one puzzle.

1   What do you get if you multiply the number in Ralph Vaughan Williams's *Parallel* in his movie music score, and the number of Mendelssohn's symphony nicknamed the 'Italian'?

2   What do you get if you multiply the number of the Mozart piano sonata that contains the *Turkish Rondo* with the number of Gorecki's *Symphony of Sorrowful Songs*?

3   What do you get if you add up the *Unforgettable* year in Shostakovich's piece that includes *The Assault on Gorky*, and the number of Beethoven's *Eroica* symphony?

4   What do you get if you multiply the number of Schubert's *Unfinished* symphony and the *Sense* in the horror movie whose soundtrack was written by prolific composers Sammy Cahn and Jule Styne?

137 MUSIC BOX

O	L	S	I	G	N
X	L	R	G	J	U
Q	A	N	R	E	S
A	A	R	O	S	S
S	U	S	I	D	A
J	O	D	E	A	B

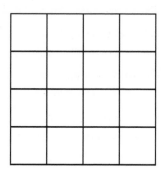

In a word square, the same words can be read both across and down. Your challenge is to create a musical word square in the empty grid using the four music-related words hidden in the letter box. The words in the letter box all appear in straight lines that can go in any direction.

138 **FORWARD PLANNING**

There are two clues to help you find two solutions. The first clue leads you to a general word. The second clue leads you to a music-based word. The solutions are very similar, but in the second word the middle letter has moved *forwards* in the alphabet.

1 Sharp sound of a switch
Nickname of Haydn's Symphony No. 101

2 A cyclist or cavalryman
Samuel Coleridge Taylor piece, *Deep* _____

3 Evergreen coniferous tree
French composer, teacher and organist Franck

4 Started, inaugurated
Soprano Mary

139 **MAJOR SEVENTH**

The classical music-related words below all contain seven letters. Put them in the grid either across or down. There is only one way to fit all the words in. One letter has been given to start you off.

ADIEMUS
BORODIN
EINAUDI
EMPEROR
FANFARE
FERRIER
GABETTA
PUCCINI
SMETANA
TOCCATA
TRIPLET
VERSION

140 **IN MY LIFETIME**

Look at these important events. What year did they take place?
Decide which of the three performers listed was alive at the time.

1 The year Neil Armstrong became the first man on the Moon.
In whose lifetime did this event take place?
a)   Francis Poulenc
b)   Igor Stravinsky
c)   Kurt Weill

2 The year the First World War began.
In whose lifetime did this event take place?
a)   Claude Debussy
b)   Nikolai Rimsky-Korsakov
c)   Gustav Mahler

3 The year that Queen Victoria came to the throne.
In whose lifetime did this event take place?
a)   Vincenzo Bellini
b)   Niccolo Paganini
c)   Franz Schubert

141 **SILENT VOICES**

The four voices that make up the four-part harmony in these vocal works have been replaced by question marks. Each question mark could be an S (soprano), A (alto), T (tenor) or B (bass). Work out the missing letters to identify the vocal works. Can you also name the composers?

1   ? H ? I ?

2   L ? ? R ? V I ? ? ?

3   P ? R ? I F ? L

4   I N P ? R ? D I ? U M

5   D I E ? O ? E ? ? ? D ?

142 **WISE WORDS**

Your challenge is to work out the hidden quotation by a Hungarian violinist and teacher.

Solve the clues and put the eight-letter answers horizontally in the first grid. Reading downwards, column A will reveal the name of the musician.

	A	B	C	D	E	F	G	H
1								
2								
3								
4								
5								
6								
7								
8								
9								
10								
11								

Use the first grid to help you complete the second one by putting in the letters that correspond to the grid coordinates. The completed second grid will reveal the rest of the quotation, which begins 'Practise with your fingers and you need all day. Practise with your mind...'.

Clues

1 Opera by Puccini first produced (but not well-received) in Turin in 1896 (2,6)
2 This Triumphal March features in Verdi's opera *Aida*
3 Samuel Barber wrote a *School for Scandal* one, and Rossini had a famous one in *The Barber of Seville*
4 Piece by Ennio Morricone, *Cinema* _____ ____
5 A piece of music such as *Judith*, *The Creation* and *Judas Maccabaeus*
6 Song from *Die Fledermaus* – designed to cheer you up?
7 The accented stroke at the beginning of a bar
8 Part of France where Canteloube's most famous folk songs came from
9 Home of Holst's most famous creations?
10 A grand arrival, such as that of the Queen of Sheba in Handel's masterpiece
11 Critic who comments on an opening performance of an opera or any musical work

B1	H2	E4		C2	H5	C6		C7	C9	A1	A6	
A7	E5		E10	G9		G1	B8	B10	E6		D11	B10
E3	B10	H4		E1	A3	A9	G3	G4				

143 NAME CHECK

```
D  B  A  G  E  L  S  Y  O  P  I  Z  N  E  Z
W  O  L  N  X  A  O  P  Y  D  E  G  E  S  I
H  R  M  V  L  Q  U  R  U  U  P  E  J  O  P
I  P  Z  E  N  O  R  A  Q  I  H  R  D  U  O
T  Y  F  I  N  A  N  R  E  Y  I  A  O  R  L
A  K  A  D  P  I  A  Z  Z  O  L  L  A  H  I
C  S  N  N  E  M  C  S  M  U  I  D  R  I  J
R  G  Z  O  U  G  R  O  W  E  P  V  T  L  A
E  R  E  X  L  F  D  W  O  S  S  O  U  M  E
J  O  L  A  O  E  I  A  H  N  Y  E  R  I  C
O  S  S  C  S  B  S  N  J  U  R  A  I  N  Y
A  S  Y  T  O  T  B  D  Z  R  B  G  R  F  L
S  U  G  H  O  R  W  E  K  I  P  E  N  A  G
L  M  U  R  O  C  I  V  O  D  U  L  R  H  M
K  H  A  C  H  A  T  U  R  I  A  N  Y  T  V
```

The first and last names of eleven composers are hidden in the word square. All words are in straight lines that run horizontally, vertically or diagonally. They may read forwards or backwards. Find all the names, then match each first name with its surname.

FIRST NAMES:

ARAM
ARTURI
ASTOR
DOMENICO
ERIC
FELA
GERALD
HUBERT
LUDOVICO
MODEST
PHILIP

SURNAMES:

EINAUDI
FINZI
GLASS
KHACHATURIAN
MARQUEZ
MUSSORGSKY
PARRY
PIAZZOLLA
SOWANDE
WHITACRE
ZIPOLI

144 SHAPE UP

In this puzzle, the letters in the names of famous composers have been replaced by symbols.

VIVALDI is

Who are the other famous names?

1

2

3

4

5

145 ON YOUR MARKS

Six young musicians have entered a competition. They all play different instruments: cello, flute, guitar, piano, trumpet and violin.

It is not easy for the judges, who are doing the best they can to judge fairly and accurately. Three new trainee assessors have been asked to give their own assessment of the musicians to compare with the judges' decisions.

Each trainee assessor is asked to name their top four of the six musicians. These are their choices:

Assessor A: The flautist first. The pianist second. The guitarist third. The trumpeter fourth.

Assessor B: The trumpeter first. The guitarist second. The violinist third. The flautist fourth.

Assessor C: The violinist first. The flautist second. The cellist third. The trumpeter fourth.

This does not quite match the judges' decisions. Of the 12 total placings by the trainees, 10 featured musicians who made the top four of the judges' selection. However, none of the three trainees have placed a musician in exactly the same position as the judges.

Which musicians appeared in the top four selected by the judges?

146 **INNER CALM**

Solve the clues. Starting in the top left-hand square of the grid, write the answers moving inwards in a clockwise direction. The words overlap with *at least* the last letter of one answer becoming the first letter of the next answer. Calmly does it!

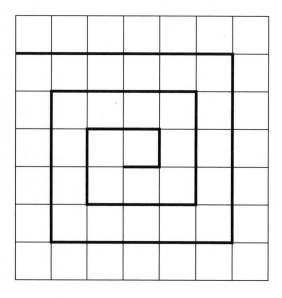

CHALLENGING PUZZLES

Clues

1 Describes Saint-Saens's *Danse*, used in the 1993 western *Tombstone*
2 The *Lacrimosa* is part of this work by Mozart
3 Title given to Beethoven's Piano Concerto No. 5
4 Surname of the Finnish conductor who is also an accomplished violinist
5 Mussorgsky's unassuming first name
6 Instruction to play each note noticeably separate
7 Music form for keyboard instruments by Widor and Bach, for example
8 Spanish composer Francisco
9 Argentine cellist Sol
10 Vaughan Williams wrote a Fantasia on his theme

147 CODA

4	■	2	■	4	18	24	4	17	4	9	10	1
1 L	2 O	3 V	4 E	■	2	■	25	■	5	■	22	■
10	■	4	■	1	10	14	22	24	13	4	9	
12	10	9	13	2	11	■	6	■	2	■	8	■
2	■	13	■	10	■	16	■	■	10	■	4	
9	2	14	16	7	■	12	2	9	2	7	6	16
10	■	9	■	■	12	2	20	■	■	2	■	23
13	24	4	10	13	9	4	■	1	10	9	22	2
4	■	8	■	■	2	■	12	■	■	10	■	19
■	1	■	8	■	15	■	9	24	19	13	24	17
21	10	16	13	10	8	6	10	■	■	6	■	4
■	26	■	10	■	4	■	3	■	13	2	15	16
9	4	21	9	4	8	24	4	7	■	16	■	13

Each letter of the alphabet has been replaced by a number. Work out which number represents which letter to complete the crossword-style grid. Words can go across or down. One word has been given to start you off.

HINTS:
The letters in two words reading across spell out famous composers. When you have cracked the code, the letter groups below name a piece of music from each composer.
12. 1. 14. 4. 12. 4. 10. 9. 7. 8 / 5. 10. 8. 13. 1. 4
18. 9. 6. 16. 5. 4 / 6. 22. 2. 9

Fill in the grid below with the letters corresponding to each number as you discover them.

1	2	3	4	5	6	7	8	9	10	11	12	13
14	15	16	17	18	19	20	21	22	23	24	25	26

148 THREE TENORS

An ambitious fantasy game intends to make full use of three operatic tenors singing the roles of the main characters. The fiction is based on Greek mythology. The lead roles are those of Apollo, Poseidon and Zeus. The characters have the same vocal range, and each role involves an equal amount of singing. The three tenors lined up are Jonas, Luciano and Roberto. There is a great deal of discussion among agents, directors and producers about how the roles will be cast. After much argument, the following five statements are agreed on by all parties.

A   Jonas will not play Zeus unless Roberto gets Apollo.
B   Luciano will not play Zeus unless Roberto gets Poseidon.
C   Jonas will not play Poseidon unless Luciano gets Zeus.
D   Roberto will not play Apollo unless Jonas gets Poseidon.
E   Jonas will not play Apollo unless Luciano gets the role of Poseidon.

What was the final casting?

149 **TRANSPOSING**

Transposing changes the pitches in a musical work without altering the relationship between the notes. Our arranger has applied the same idea to the lyrics!

Each letter of the alphabet has changed position and the change is consistent for every letter, so if A was transposed to B, B would become C, C would become D, and so on.

Here are the words of a stirring popular song after the letters have been transposed. Work out the transposition rule to read the lyrics.

HINTS: Shorter words can provide a clue as there are less options that they could be. Also, look for letters that appear together and at the frequency of individual letters. Do the punctuation marks help?

GVIY / JA / CJKZ / VIY / BGJMT,
HJOCZM / JA / OCZ / AMZZ,
CJR / NCVGG / RZ / ZSOJG / OCZZ,
RCJ / VMZ / WJMI / JA / OCZZ?

150 **CRYPTIC**

A cryptic crossword to massage the mind.

Across

1 Trout and variations in Puccini opera (8)

7 Record but not a collection, that would be one for stamps (5)

8 Continuous thread the mezzosoprano delivered (5)

9 Actors regroup to come up with top leading man or lady (2-4)

10 Describes blonde at Delius's event at *Brigg* (4)

12 Sounds correct at Stravinsky's *Spring* masterpiece (4)

14 John Williams's *Hymn* to them, who weren't those who had lost their reputation (6)

17 Sounds like a catalogue of items regarding this Hungarian composer (5)

18 Shards of amber light up this guitarist (5)

19 Sit sharp as these instrumentalists come in to the spotlight (8)

Down

1 Abuts new arrivals in the brass section (5)

2 The kind of aura me 'not you' produce around French composer (6)

3 Change of tone produces a sound (4)

4 Her scope ranges from oratorio to comedy, it would appear (5)

5 Song from *The Gondoliers* or just from gondoliers? (9)

6 Sounds like this goblin in the underground helps keep time (9)

11 Bass ma invented for Brazilian dances (6)

13 Leave coats behind at this operatic performance (5)

15 Goes in front at this competition venue it is said (5)

16 Put an end to organ control (4)

GENTLE
SOLUTIONS

1 KEY-BOARD

mn	D	A	G	F	E	mj	B	C
mj	F	B	C	D	A	mn	E	G
E	C	G	B	mj	mn	A	F	D
C	E	F	A	mn	B	G	D	mj
G	A	D	mj	E	C	F	mn	B
B	mj	mn	D	G	F	C	A	E
A	G	E	F	C	D	B	mj	mn
D	B	mj	mn	A	G	E	C	F
F	mn	C	E	B	mj	D	G	A

2 MINDFULNESS

The five letters that do not appear in the box are E, F, L, T and U.

The musical instrument is FLUTE.

3 EASE INTO EIGHT

1   Concerts (A)
2   Electric (A)
3   Triangle (A)
4   Accolade (C)
5   Folk song (C)
6   Sopranos (A)
7   Flamenco (A)
8   American (C)

4 IN THE SHADE

1   Bohemia
2   Florida
3   Quartet
4   Richard
5   Prodigy
6   Belfast
7   Working
8   Theatre
9   Invited
10   Conduct

The end of the quotation is: *both of which I try to avoid.*

5 LENTO

Across

6 Double
7 Diva
9 Encore
10 Leeds
12 Reed
13 Pedal
17 Opera
18 Lute
21 Viola
22 Anthem
24 Item
25 Minute

Down

1 Quintet
2 Alto
3 William
4 Wales
5 Brass
8 Rehearsal
11 Art
14 Speaker
15 Tuneful
16 Met
19 Ivory
20 Movie
23 Trio

6 CHILL OUT

1 Concertina
2 Harmonica
3 Clarinet
4 Piccolo
5 Chimes
6 Cello

7 TIME LAG

Sandra is 40 and Millie is 10. Sandra is four times as old as her daughter. In 20 years, Sandra will be 60 and Millie 30. Millie will then be half as old as her mother.

8 LET GO

1   Let go of cuckoo, lark and nightingale
2   Let go of anthem, air, ditty, hymn, aria
3   Let go of hill, headland, mountain, peak, tor
4   Let go of tricolour, tripod, trio, triangle, triplet
5   Let go of flute (lute), sharp (harp), thorn (horn), organise (organ)
6   Let go of Pavlova (meringue dessert named after ballerina Anna) and Melba (Peach Melba named after opera singer Dame Nellie Melba)
7   Let go of bear, cat, mouse, monkey, tiger, lion.

The title of the piece of music is *Swan Lake* (Tchaikovsky).

9 **SOFTLY**

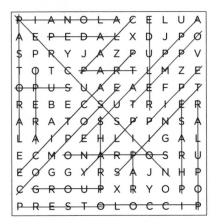

10 **DUOS**

First on stage are Paul and Nigella.
Second to sing are George and Paula.
Finally, Nigel and Georgina sing their duet.

11 MISSING FROM THE MOVIES

1 *West Side Story*
2 *Les Misérables*
3 *Titanic*
4 *Ladies in Lavender*
5 *The Great Escape*

12 STAR GAZING

1 Gardner
2 Einaudi
3 Rossini
4 Gabetta
5 Vivaldi
6 Corelli
7 Sowande

The ballet is *Giselle*.

13 NUMBER NAMES

R = 1
I = 2
A = 3
O = 4
D = 5

As AIR = 6, the individual letters must be 1, 2 and 3 in any order. Both AIR and IDA contain an A and an I. The difference between the word totals must be the difference between letter R and D. D is worth four more than R. Therefore, D equals 5 and R equals 1. AIDA contains the same letters as IDA plus another A. A must equal the difference between totals. 13 – 10 = 3. In AIR, R = 1 and A = 3, leaving I as 2. All numbers are allocated except 4 which must be O.

14 CLOUD NINE

a)   TAPE
b)   CAST
c)   DIRECT

The word in the grid is PRACTISED.

15 **BEHIND THE SCENES**

1 Elgar
2 Handel
3 Chopin
4 Verdi

16 **HAVE A BREAK**

1 *Swan Lake*
2 *Peer Gynt*
3 *Water Music*

17 **WHAT AM I?**

SHARP

18 **BLOWING BUBBLES**

The question mark is the letter E.
Top left: Trumpeter
Top right: Drummer
Bottom: Composer

19 HALF FULL?

1 Echo
2 Hope
3 Peal
4 Alto
5 Tour

20 RING CYCLE

1 Suffolk
2 Karaoke
3 *Emperor*
4 Refrain
5 Needles

21 **SMOOTHIE**

Simon has spent 10 hours listening to music. Violin music took up a quarter of the day, which is the same as 25%. Add this to the 40% spent listening to piano music to get 65%. That leaves 35% of time spent with Gregorian chants and the guitar. Three hours plus half an hour was the combined times meaning that three and a half hours equals 35% of Simon's listening time. Divide by 35 and multiply by 100 to find 100%, which is 10 hours.

22 **HALL OF FAME**

114 records are on their way down. There are 30 non-movers + 130 moving up from last year + 26 brand new entries = 186. 300 – 186 = 114.

23 PERFECT FIFTH

1 March
3 Octet
5 Beats
7 Strum
9 Tutor
11 Vocal

24 SIXTH SENSE

1 Rattle
2 Learnt
3 Troupe
4 Saturn
5 Studio
6 Volume
7 Career
8 Tattoo
9 Queued
10 Guitar
11 Centre
12 Encore

25 HONEYCOMB

1 Finale
2 Player
3 Priest
4 Museum
5 Hummed
6 Oldest
7 London
8 Melody
9 Naples
10 Danced
11 Fiddle
12 Eiffel

26 TAKE NOTE

Words in order: DOUBLE, ANGLAIS, ELECTRIC, BASS, COR, GUITAR

They pair up as: COR ANGLAIS, DOUBLE BASS, ELECTRIC GUITAR

27 CAR RIDE

1 Oscar
2 Red carpet
3 *Carmen*
4 Caruso
5 Carnation
6 Cartoon

28 TO THE POINT

1 Tour
2 *Free*
3 Tune
4 Veto
5 Test
6 Ends
7 Rome
8 Item
9 Isle
10 Idol

29 TAKE FIVE

C	H	O	I	R
A		P		E
R	E	E	D	S
O		R		T
L	E	A	D	S

30 FILLERS

1   TONE (STONES, BARITONE, ATONED
2   PLAY (REPLAY, PLAYGROUND, DISPLAY)
3   BOW (ELBOW, BOWLING, BOWLER)

31 **COMPOSE YOURSELF**

JENKINS is formed in the shaded diagonal.

1   Janáček
2   Berlioz
3   Einaudi
4   Busking
5   Puccini
6   Harmony
7   Octaves

32 **BAX WORDS**

1   Brahms
2   Bach
3   Mozart
4   Holst

33 MOVIE A TO Z

1 *Wilde* (Debbie Wiseman)
2 *The Mission* (Ennio Morricone)
3 *The Great Escape* (Elmer Bernstein)
4 *Gladiator* (Hans Zimmer)

34 MY MISTAKE

1 Star Ward (*Star Wars*)
2 Rome Alone (*Home Alone*)
3 Superfan (*Superman*)

35 REARRANGEMENT

1 Drive and Verdi
2 Large and Elgar
3 Handy and Haydn
4 Handle and Handel
5 Horse and Shore

36 LUCKY NUMBERS

1 *Born on the Fourth of July* and *The Magnificent Seven* = 4 x 7 = 28
2 *2001: A Space Odyssey* and two gangs (the Sharks and the Jets) in *West Side Story* = 2001 x 2 = 4002
3 Performers in a sestet = 6 and letters of the alphabet on a piano keyboard = 7 = 6 x 7 = 42
4 Turtle doves delivered on the second day of Christmas = 2 and performers in three trios = 9 = 2 x 9 = 18

37 **MUSIC BOX**

F	L	A	T
L	Y	R	E
A	R	T	S
T	E	S	T

38 **FORWARD PLANNING**

1. Chair and choir
2. Baron and baton
3. Quakers and quavers
4. Wafer and *Water*

39 **IN MY LIFETIME**

1   England won the football World Cup in 1966. This took place in Bryn Terfel's lifetime (born 1965).

2   The Channel Tunnel opened in 1994. This took place in Nicola Benedetti's lifetime (born 1987).

3   *The Good, the Bad and the Ugly* was released in 1966. This took place in Nigel Kennedy's lifetime (born 1957).

40 **MAJOR SEVENTH**

41 **WISE WORDS**

1 Serenade
2 Clarinet
3 Handbell
4 Organist
5 Enjoying
6 Nocturne
7 Baritone
8 Ensemble
9 Rhapsody
10 Gravelly

The composer is Schoenberg.

He describes Webern's *Six Bagatelles* as 'a novel in a single gesture, a joy in a breath.'

42 **INSTRUMENTS**

43 **SILENT VOICES**

1 *Messiah*
2 *Tosca*
3 *Aida*
4 *Lacrimosa*
5 *Ave Maria*

44 **PROMISING SIGNS**

1 Aries
2 Scorpio
3 Capricorn
4 Aquarius
5 Sagittarius

45 INNER CALM

1 Singer
2 *Rings*
3 Seal
4 Alan (Titchmarsh)
5 *Animals*
6 Sell out
7 Te Kanawa
8 Waltzing
9 Glass
10 Soloist

46 CODA

Code: 1/A, 2/R, 3/T, 4/S, 5/H, 6/E, 7/V, 8/J, 9/C, 10/O, 11/N, 12/D, 13/F, 14/Q, 15/P, 16/W, 17/K, 18/Z, 19/I, 20/Y, 21/G, 22/X, 23/U, 24/M, 25/L, 26/B

Left to right and top to bottom of the grid:

ACROSS: Beethoven, arts, playback, market, nears, request, mud, sweeten, piece, invent, tutorial, echo, xylophone.

DOWN: harmonise, stargazer, empty, thanked, orbs, each, reference, attention, run, messiah, Milan, jury, solo.

Moonlight Sonata is the coded piece of work by Beethoven.

47 PERSONAL CHOICE

Everyone has chosen an instrument that contains the letters in their name, so Tom will choose the trombone.

48 ADDERS

1   TRUMP + ET = TRUMPET
2   RAG + TIME = RAGTIME
3   BAG + PIPES = BAGPIPES
4   KEY + BOARD = KEYBOARD
5   WISE + MAN = WISEMAN (Debbie)

49 E-E-EASY DOES IT

```
B                 R           G     T
O   P A R R Y     R       Z   L     A
R   I       P U C C I N I  I  A     L
O   A       C           P     S     L
D   Z   B R A H M S   R O S S I N I I
F I N Z I           M     L         S
  N     O   R A C H M A N I N O F F
A       L           A   S
R       L   B A R R Y   C O P L A N D
M O Z A R T       D     A
S       C H O P I N   G I U R I O L I
T       H           N
R       V A U G H A N W I L L I A M S
O R F F I           A         L
N       K O R N G O L D   B A C H
G       O           T     I     O
  P     V           O Q U I N N   L
  A   S C H U M A N N       O     S
D V O R A K               N     T
  T     Y                 I
```

50 CRYPTIC

Across

1 Falsetto
7 Roles
8 Dance
9 Hosted
10 Trio
12 Spin
14 Ballad
17 Raise
18 Choir
19 Whistles

Down

1 Films
2 Listen
3 Ends
4 Tenor
5 Orchestra
6 Recorders
11 Cancel
13 Irish
15 Lions
16 Keys

MODERATE
SOLUTIONS

51 KEY-BOARD

F	G	B	E	C	D	mj	mn	A
E	A	mj	mn	G	B	C	F	D
mn	D	C	mj	A	F	B	E	G
B	mn	D	F	mj	A	E	G	C
mj	C	A	G	E	mn	D	B	F
G	E	F	B	D	C	mn	A	mj
A	mj	E	C	mn	G	F	D	B
C	B	G	D	F	E	A	mj	mn
D	F	mn	A	B	mj	G	C	E

52 MINDFULNESS

The five letters that do not appear in the box are C, G, L, K and U.

The composer is GLUCK.

53 EASE INTO EIGHT

1   Bass drum (C)
2   Recorder (A)
3   Bagpipes (C)
4   Concerto (C)
5   Operetta (A)
6   Schubert (A)
7   Trombone (C)
8   *Iolanthe* (C)

54 IN THE SHADE

1   Bassoon
2   Playing
3   Records
4   Hungary
5   Finnish
6   Cellist
7   Academy
8   Maracas
9   Ukulele
10   Cornets

The full quotation is: *My music is best understood by children and animals.*

55 **LENTO**

Across

6 Voices
7 Bell
9 *Danube*
10 India
12 Ends
13 Italy
17 Aaron
18 *Blue*
21 Swing
22 Edward
24 Clap
25 Cradle

Down

1 Vivaldi
2 Peru
3 Seville
4 Slide
5 Elgar
8 Beethoven
11 *New*
14 Vaughan
15 Florida
16 Key
19 Psalm
20 Pitch
23 Work

56 **CHILL OUT**

1 Carillon
2 Capriccio
3 Chromatic
4 Pitch
5 Plainchant
6 Octachord

57 **RETRO**

Julie must sell 11 more records. She is selling them for £2 each. The scores cost £4. She needs to sell one record to break even and ten more to get her takings to £20.

58 **SEARCH FOR CALM**

HARMONY does not appear in the word box.

59 LET GO

1   Let go of Sousa (sousaphone), Sax (saxophone), Moog (moog synthesiser)
2   Let go of Bliss, Rossini and Britten
3   Let go of zither, kazoo, bazooka
4   Let go of cello, guitar, viola, lute
5   Let go of five, eight, six, seven
6   Let go of waltz, tango, polka, jive, rumba
7   Let go of wedding, anniversary, birthday
8   Let go of Wagner, Bartók, Mozart, Chopin and Liszt.

The piece of music is Vivaldi's *Four Seasons*.

60 HAPPY BIRTHDAY

There are 15 people in the choir. Ten ladies and five gentlemen. Each member sends out 5 cards, 14 to fellow singers plus one to the musical director. They don't send themselves a card!

61 MISSING FROM THE MOVIES

1 *Saving Private Ryan*
2 *Raiders of the Lost Ark*
3 *Home Alone*
4 *War Horse*
5 *War of the Worlds*

The composer is John Williams.

62 STAR GAZING

1 Whistle
2 Piccolo
3 Bassoon
4 Laments
5 Drummer
6 Recital
7 Refrain

The composer is Debbie WISEMAN.

63 NUMBER NAMES

TRUMPET = 31

E = 1
P = 2
O = 3
M = 4
U = 5
T = 6
R = 7

The four letters in POEM must be 1, 2, 3 and 4, in any order. That is the only combination of different numbers to add up to 10. Both MORE and PROM contain the letters M, O and R. The difference between them is a letter E in the former and a P in the latter. It follows that P = E + 1. Both POEM and PROM contain the letters M, O, P. The difference between them is E in the former and R in the latter. The difference in word value is 16 – 10 = 6. Therefore R must be six greater than E, making R 7 and E 1. The value of P can now be fixed as it equals E (1) + 1 = 2. The word TEMPO contains the letters in POEM plus a T. T is the difference between the two values. 16 – 10 = 6. In MUTE, the value of T is 6, E is 1. Take these away from MUTE to leave M and U with a combined value of 9. The only option available is for M to be worth 4 and U to be worth 5.

64 CLOUD NINE

a) SOLO
b) FLUTE
c) KNELL

The phrase in the grid is FOLK TUNES.

65 BEHIND THE SCENES

1 Gluck
2 Lehár
3 Delius
4 Satie

66 HAVE A BREAK

1 *Eugene Onegin*
2 *Lakmé, Tosca*
3 Carmen, Figaro

67 **WHAT AM I?**

RADIO

The first letter could be E or R. The second letter has more options and could be A, E, R or T. The third letter could be D or I. The fourth letter could be I or L. The fifth letter has to be an O. The only combination of letters to make a word spells out RADIO.

68 **BLOWING BUBBLES**

The question mark is the letter M.
Top left: (Freddie) De Tommaso
Top right: (Placido) Domingo
Bottom: (Roderick) Williams

69 **HALF FULL?**

1 Riga
2 Gala
3 Lara (*Lara's Theme*)
4 Ravi
5 Viol

70 **RING CYCLE**

1 Soloist
2 Toccata
3 Allegro
4 *October*
5 Rhythms

71 **SOUNDTRACK**

All items have their chart placing featured in the title.
ONE is formed by linking NO NEVER.
TWO is formed by linking LAST WOMAN.
THREE is formed by linking WITH REELS.
FOUR is formed by linking INFO URGENTLY.

72 **IN TRAINING**

She lives 12 miles from the opera house. She is out for a total of 5 hours. It takes 2 hours to get from home to the opera house when running (2 x 6 = 12). It takes 3 hours to make the return journey while speed walking (3 x 4 = 12).

73 PERFECT FIFTH

1   Viola
3   Elgar
5   Major
7   Holst
9   Ascot
11 Tonic

74 TAKE NOTE

Words in order: ORFF, *SIEGFRIED,* VERDI, *CARMINA BURANA,*
WAGNER, *AIDA*
They pair up as: ORFF *CARMINA BURANA,* VERDI *AIDA,* WAGNER
SIEGFRIED

75 **SIXTH SENSE**

1 Summer
2 French
3 Cycles
4 Caruso
5 Unison
6 Throat
7 Murray
8 Launch
9 Albums
10 Norman
11 Brahms
12 Cornet

76 **HONEYCOMB**

1 Summer (c)
2 Pipers (a)
3 Chopin (c)
4 Choral (a)
5 Horner (c)
6 Verses (a)
7 Wolves (a)
8 Violin (c)
9 Violas (a)
10 Walton (a)
11 Presto (c)
12 Zimmer (c)

77 FIND HER

1 *The Pearl Fishers*
2 *Albert Herring*
3 Zither
4 Herbert von Karajan
5 Scherzo
6 (Bernard) Herrmann

78 TO THE POINT

1 Karl
2 Blog
3 Trio
4 Ugly
5 Noel
6 Live
7 Hymn
8 *Plum*
9 Peru
10 Ever

79 TAKE FIVE

D	U	K	A	S
E		I		T
B	I	N	G	E
U		G		V
T	A	S	T	E

80 FILLERS

1 HEAR (REHEARSE, SHEARS, HEARSAY)
2 AIR (STAIRS, FLAIR, FAIRWAY)
3 LUTE (FLUTE, GLUTEN, DILUTED)

81 **COMPOSE YOURSELF**

TIPPETT is formed in the shaded diagonal.

1 Tavener
2 Wiseman
3 Reprise
4 Vespers
5 Cornets
6 Andante
7 Quartet

82 **BAX WORDS**

1 Fauré
2 Pärt
3 Wiseman
4 Widor

83 MOVIE A TO Z

1   *Raiders of the Lost Ark* (John Williams)
2   *The Magnificent Seven* (Elmer Bernstein)
3   *The Lord of the Rings* (Howard Shore)
4   *Sherlock Holmes* (Hans Zimmer)

84 MY MISTAKE

1   Hairy Potter (*Harry Potter*)
2   Jurassic Pork (*Jurassic Park*)
3   Indiana Bones (*Indiana Jones*)

85 REARRANGEMENT

1 Laver and Ravel
2 Near and Arne
3 Sloth and Holst
4 Bittern and Britten
5 Ronald and Arnold

86 LUCKY NUMBERS

1 *Choral Symphony* = 9 and Years in Tibet = 7 = 9 x 7 = 63
2 *Four Last Songs* – one opera by Beethoven (*Fidelio*) = 4 – 1 = 3
3 Add all the digits in 1812 to make 12
4 *Apollo 13* + 60 seconds = 73

87 MUSIC BOX

A	L	T	O
L	O	U	D
T	U	N	E
O	D	E	S

88 FORWARD PLANNING

1 Bless and Bliss
2 Elder and Elmer
3 Unbar and Ungar
4 Share and Shore

89 IN MY LIFETIME

1 The first Academy Awards ceremony took place in 1929. This was in Aaron Copland's lifetime (1900–1990).

2 Classic FM was founded in 1992. This was in Harrison Birtwistle's lifetime (1934–2022).

3 Queen Elizabeth II's Silver Jubilee was in 1977. This was in Lesley Garrett's lifetime (born 1955).

90 MAJOR SEVENTH

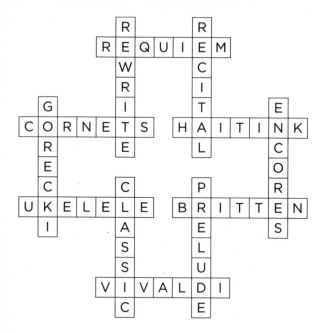

91 WISE WORDS

1   Bass drum
2   Eighteen (*1812 Overture*)
3   *New World*
4   Entr'acte
5   Dominant
6   Emphasis
7   Trombone
8   Triangle
9   Identify

The name of the musician is violinist (Nicola) Benedetti.

Her advice to musicians is: 'Focus on those one or two notes and get that ringing quality and *your ears will start to demand more of the same.*'

92 ON GOOD TERMS

The word PRESTO appears twice.

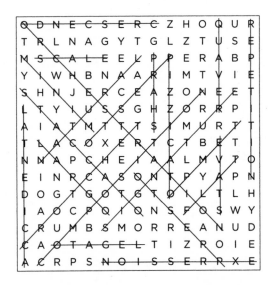

93 SILENT VOICES

1   *Faust*
2   *Macbeth*
3   *Tannhauser*
4   *Rusalka*
5   *Turandot*

94 SHAPE UP

1   Lehár
2   Handel
3   Verdi
4   Mahler
5   Bellini

95 LIKES

He had 80 likes at the end of day 1.
80 likes at the end of day 1.
60 more on day 2, giving 140 for the day and a running total of 220.
60 increase on day 3, giving 200 for the day and running total of 420.
60 increase on day 4, giving 260 for the day and a running total of 680.
60 increase on day 5, giving 320 for the day and a running total of 1,000.

96 INNER CALM

1   Gillam
2   *American*
3   Andante
4   Terfel
5   Felicity
6   Yodel
7   Delilah
8   Haitink
9   Korngold
10 Day

97 **CODA**

Code: 1/T, 2/R, 3/U, 4/E, 5/H, 6/S, 7/Y, 8/C, 9/N, 10/A, 11/G, 12/V, 13/M, 14/Z, 15/D, 16/B, 17/O, 18/F, 19/J, 20/I, 21/X, 22/W, 23/Q, 24/P, 25/K, 26/L

Left to right and top to bottom of the grid:

ACROSS: quarterly, true, tapestry, notice, reply, premier, sat, respond, speak, belief, arpeggio, shoe, edelweiss

DOWN: itinerary, juxtapose, utter, rapport, easy, lyre, limelight, Prokofiev, pad, snuggle, oboes, grid, zeal.

The Love for Three Oranges is the coded piece of work by Prokofiev.

98 **ADDERS**

1   APP + LAUD = APPLAUD
2   HAND + EL = HANDEL
3   UNI + SON = UNISON
4   COP + LAND = COPLAND
5   REF + RAIN = REFRAIN

99 **TRANSPOSING**

ONCE IN ROYAL DAVID'S CITY,
STOOD A LOWLY CATTLE SHED,
WHERE A MOTHER LAID HER BABY,
IN A MANGER FOR HIS BED.

A has transposed to E, meaning that all letters move four places in the alphabet: A becomes E, B becomes F, C becomes G, and so on.

100 **CRYPTIC**

Across

1 Schubert
7 Ad lib
8 Range
9 Master
10 Horn
12 Nine
14 Dulcet
17 Coral
18 Verdi
19 *Pastoral*

Down

1 Solos
2 Hebrew
3 Byrd
4 Rondo
5 Harmonica
6 Bernstein
11 Quaver
13 *Norma*
15 Carol
16 Flat

CHALLENGING
SOLUTIONS

101 **KEY-BOARD**

F	G	C	E	mj	D	B	mn	A
mj	D	B	A	mn	C	F	G	E
E	A	mn	B	G	F	D	mj	C
mn	C	mj	G	D	B	A	E	F
D	E	A	F	C	mn	G	B	mj
G	B	F	mj	A	E	mn	C	D
C	mn	D	mn	B	A	E	F	G
A	mn	E	C	F	G	mj	D	B
B	F	G	D	E	mj	C	A	mn

102 **MINDFULNESS**

The five letters that do not appear in the box are A, G, I, N and P.
The A, N and I are used twice to form the composer's name PAGANINI.

103 **EASE INTO EIGHT**

1 Paganini (C)
2 Sibelius (C)
3 *Taverner* (A)
4 Mascagni (A)
5 Mandolin (C)
6 *Agnus Dei* (A)
7 Albinoni (C)
8 Woodwind (C)

104 **IN THE SHADE**

1 Oratorio
2 Schubert
3 Sinfonia
4 *Squadron*
5 *Iolanthe*
6 Soh / Film
7 Tranquil
8 Chansons
9 Clementi
10 Sequence

The quotation reads: *This is the sound of nature not music.*

105 **LENTO**

Across

6 Cuckoo (*On Hearing the First Cuckoo in Spring*)
7 Eric (Coates)
9 Sonata
10 Milan
12 Glee
13 Motet
17 Eight
18 Dido (*Dido and Aeneas*)
21 Lehár
22 Norman
24 Mute
25 Sleigh (*Sleigh Ride*)

Down

1 October
2 Jota
3 Trumpet
4 Scale
5 Chant
8 Saxophone
11 Age
14 Vibrato
15 Titania (*A Midsummer Night's Dream*)
16 *Toy*
19 Bliss
20 Chime
23 Rule (*Rule Britannia*)

106 **CHILL OUT**

1 Puccini (Giacomo)
2 Cherubini (Luigi)
3 Boccherini (Luigi)
4 Ponchielli (Amilcare)
5 Locatelli (Pietro)
6 Dallapiccola (Luigi)

There are three composers with the first name LUIGI.

107 **PASSCODE**

5274163. If 1 was the final digit, the penultimate digit would need to be 2 to be double the 1. This cannot be the case, as there has to be difference of more than one between adjacent digits. If the final digit is 2, the penultimate has to be 4. The four odd digits need placing in five spaces without any two odd numbers being adjacent, which is impossible. 3 is the last digit and 6 is the penultimate digit. As 3 is an odd number, it follows that the first, third and fifth letters must be odd to avoid odd numbers appearing side by side. Neither 5 nor 7 is more than 1 greater than 6. Only 1 is left. The number in front of 1 has to be even and it cannot be 2, leaving only the 4. 5 cannot go next to 4, so 7 must. The remaining even number, 2, is fixed as the second digit leaving 5 as the opening digit in the number.

108 **FAR, FAR AWAY**

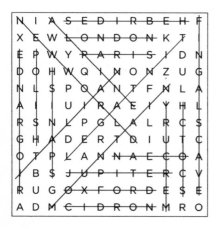

The unused letters spell out FLORIDA, where Frederick Delius lived for a while on an orange plantation.

109 **LET GO**

1   Let go of Britten, Messiaen, Rutter, Walton and Jenkins.
2   Let go of Bax, Ravel and Gounod (x = 10, l = 50, d = 500)
3   Let go of Georges Bizet, Gioacchino Rossini, Frederick Delius, Alexander Borodin and Wolfgang Amadeus Mozart.
4   Let go of Arnold, Orff and Verdi.
5   Let go of Henry Purcell, Edward Elgar, Richard Wagner and William Byrd.
6   Let go of Elijah, Job, Joseph, Judith and Samson.
7   Let go of Benedetti, Grappelli, Menuhin and Paganini.

The piece of music is *Upside Down Violin* by Michael Nyman.

110 **SING ALONG**

They disband. Attendance numbers are determined by how many letters are used to spell out the previous number when written as a word. Twenty-eight contains 11 letters. The word eleven contains six letters. The word six contains three letters. The word three contains five letters. The word five contains four letters, so that determines only four singers attend the final meeting.

111 MISSING FROM THE MOVIES

1 *Gladiator*
2 *The Last Samurai*
3 *Interstellar*
4 *No Time To Die*
5 *Angels and Demons*

The composer is Hans Zimmer.

112 STAR GAZING

Names: Placido Domingo, John Tavener, Michael Tippett, Kathleen Ferrier, Andrés Segovia, Montserrat Caballé, Joaquín Rodrigo
Grid placing: 1 Ferrier, 2 Tippett, 3 Rodrigo, 4 Tavener, 5 Caballé, 6 Segovia, 7 Domingo

The opera is *Fidelio* by Beethoven.

113 NUMBER NAMES

CLASSIC = 30

A = 1
R = 2
I = 3
S = 4
C = 5
N = 6
M = 7
L = 8

If ARIAS = 11, then A must be 1, with I, R, S as 2, 3, 4 in any combination. MASS = 16. Take away the A (value 1) and 15 is the total of M + S + S. S is 2, 3 or 4. The only combination to make 15 is if S = 4 and M = 7. In CALLS, the value of A and S is known. Take away those letters (1 and 4) and the value of C + L + L = 21 (26 – 1 – 4). C has to be 5 and L has to be 8. MARIA CALLAS and LA SCALA MILAN are remarkably similar in the letters they use. The former is made up of 11 letters: A, A, A, A, C, I, L, L, M, R, S. The latter is made up of 12 letters: A, A, A, A, C, I, L, L, L, M, N, S. The only difference is that the singer's name includes an R and the opera house's name contains an extra L and an N. The difference between name values is 12 (53 – 41). The letter L is worth 8, so the N has to be four more than the letter R, which is established as being either 2 or 3. If R was 3 then N would be 3 + 4 = 7. M has a value of 7, so R must be 2 and N 6. I is left with a value of 3.

114 CLOUD NINE

a) TOY
b) ACCENT
c) STOPS

The word in the grid is SYNCOPATE.

115 BEHIND THE SCENES

1 Arne
2 Cage
3 Widor
4 Smyth

116 HAVE A BREAK

1 *Fidelio, Nabucco*
2 *Gloriana, Turandot*
3 *Falstaff, Parsifal*

117 **WHAT AM I?**

THEATRE. The first letter has to be T and the second letter is H. The third letter could be A or E. The fourth letter has more options and could be A, E or R. The fifth letter could be A or T. The sixth letter has to be R. The final letter has to be E. The only combination of letters to make a word spells out THEATRE.

118 **BLOWING BUBBLES**

The question mark is the letter D.
Top left: *The Armed Man*.
Top right: *Palladio*.
Bottom: *Adiemus*.
The composer is Sir Karl Jenkins.

119 **HALF FULL?**

1 Paco (Pena)
2 Coda
3 Dais
4 *Isle (of the Dead)*
5 *(King) Lear*

120 **RING CYCLE**

1 Scherzo
2 Offbeat
3 Timpani
4 *Italian*
5 Neuhaus

121 COMMITTEE MEETING

Andrea is the Chair. Moving in a clockwise direction, Dave is Membership Secretary. Carol is Treasurer. Phil is the Artistic Director. Julie is the Social Secretary.

122 TOKEN GESTURE

The festival-goer saw seven Band A performances. These used seven tokens. Three concerts were seen at Band B using nine tokens. Two concerts were seen at Band C using eight tokens. 7 + 9 + 8 is the only combination to see 12 events with 24 tokens.

123 PERFECT FIFTH

1 Parry
3 *Armed*
5 Weill
7 Altos
9 Sound
11 Ungar

124 TAKE NOTE

Words in order: BEAR, DELIUS, *ADELAIDE,* HAYDN, *BRIGG FAIR,* BEETHOVEN

They pair up as: BEETHOVEN *ADELAIDE* (cantata), DELIUS *BRIGG FAIR* (rhapsody), HAYDN *BEAR* (symphony)

125 SIXTH SENSE

1   Wagner
2   (The) Mikado
3   Herald
4   George
5   Handel
6   Louise
7   Marine
8   Legato
9   Madrid
10 Vienna
11 (Malcolm) Arnold
12 (Dame) Nellie (Melba)

126 HONEYCOMB

1   Gerald (Finzi) (a)
2   Bridge (c)
3   Irving (Berlin) (a)
4   Singer (a)
5   Angela (a)
6   Africa (a)
7   France (a)
8   Carmen (a)
9   Mozart (a)
10 Thomas (Tallis) (a)
11 Thames (a)
12 Rameau (a)

127 TIN MINING

1 Concertina
2 Martinu
3 *Tintagel*
4 Martini
5 Austin Friars
6 *Cavatina*

128 TO THE POINT

1 Troy
2 Hyde
3 Loud
4 Beat
5 Idea
6 *Duke*
7 Styx
8 *Lady*
9 Reed
10 Skye

129 **TAKE FIVE**

130 **FILLERS**

1 READ (THREAD, BREAD and DREADED)
2 REST (CREST, RESTORE, ARRESTING)
3 HARP (HARPOON, SHARPEN, HARPY)

131 **COMPOSE YOURSELF**

SALIERI is formed in the shaded diagonal.

1 Smetana
2 *Janáček*
3 Ballads
4 Recital
5 Poulenc
6 Koshiro
7 Vivaldi

132 **BAX WORDS**

1 Rossini
2 Bruch
3 Mahler
4 Allegri

133 MOVIE A TO Z

1 *An American In Paris* (George Gershwin)
2 *To Kill a Mockingbird* (Elmer Bernstein)
3 *On Her Majesty's Secret Service* (John Barry)
4 *The Dark Knight* (Hans Zimmer)

134 MY MISTAKE

1 The Umpire Strikes Back (*The Empire Strikes Back*)
2 Caving Private Ryan (*Saving Private Ryan*)
3 Close Encounters of the Third King (*Close Encounters of the Third Kind*).

135 REARRANGEMENT

1   Harlem and Mahler
2   Butchers and Schubert
3   Collier and Corelli
4   Retsina and Stainer
5   Tameness and Massenet

136 LUCKY NUMBERS

1   *Parallel 49* and Mendelssohn's Symphony No. 4 = 49 x 4 = 196
2   Mozart's *Piano Sonata No. 11* and Gorecki's Symphony No. 3 = 11 x 3 = 33
3   Shostakovich's *Unforgettable* year was 1919 and the *Eroica* is No 3, 1919 + 3 = 1922
4   Schubert's *Unfinished* symphony is No. 8 and *The Sixth Sense* = 8 x 6 = 48

137 **MUSIC BOX**

B	A	S	S
A	R	I	A
S	I	G	N
S	A	N	G

138 **FORWARD PLANNING**

1 Click and *Clock*
2 Rider and River
3 Cedar and César
4 Began and Bevan

139 MAJOR SEVENTH

```
        T           E
    B O R O D I N
        C           N
        C           A
  F     A           U         P
G A B E T T A   A D I E M U S
  N     A           I         C
  F                           C
  A     F           E         I
T R I P L E T   S M E T A N A
  E     R           P         I
        R           E
        I           R
    V E R S I O N
        R           R
```

140 IN MY LIFETIME

1 Neil Armstrong became the first man on the Moon in 1969. This was in Igor Stravinsky's lifetime (1882–1971).

2 The First World War began in 1914. This was in Claude Debussy's lifetime (1862–1918).

3 Queen Victoria came to the throne in 1837. This was in Niccolo Paganini's lifetime (1782–1840).

141 SILENT VOICES

1 *Thais* (Massenet)
2 *La Traviata* (Verdi)
3 *Parsifal* (Wagner)
4 *In Paradisum* (Eimear Quinn)
5 *Die Tote Stadt* (Korngold)

142 WISE WORDS

1 *La bohème*
2 Egyptian
3 Overture
4 *Paradiso*
5 Oratorio
6 *(The) Laughing (Song)*
7 Downbeat
8 Auvergne
9 Universe
10 Entrance
11 Reviewer

The name of the Hungarian violinist and teacher is Leopold Auer.

He said: 'Practise with your fingers and you need all day. Practise with your mind *and you will do as much in two hours.*'

143 NAME CHECK

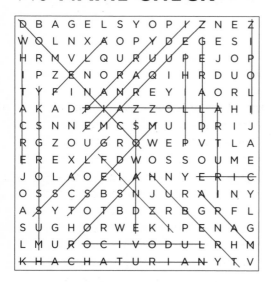

The names pair up as follows:

Aram Khachaturian

Arturi Marquez

Astor Piazzolla

Domenico Zipoli

Eric Whitacre

Fela Sowande

Gerald Finzi

Hubert Parry

Ludovico Einaudi

Modest Mussorgsky

Philip Glass

144 SHAPE UP

1 Einaudi

2 Albinoni

3 Borodin

4 Rossini

5 Addinsell

145 **ON YOUR MARKS**

1st = guitarist
2nd = trumpeter
3rd = flautist
4th = violinist

The trainee assessors have made a total of 12 placings. These break down to three for both the flautist and the trumpeter, two for the guitarist and the violinist, with one each for the cellist and the pianist. As 10 of the 2 musicians featured in the judges' marking, there is no combination in which the musicians with a single placing can appear. The ten are made up of the four musicians who were placed twice or three times. Sadly, the cellist and pianist can be discounted from the judges' results. The flautist was given a first, second and fourth placing by the trainees, and as none gave a correct position, the flautist has to be placed third by the judges. For the same reasoning, the trumpeter has to be second. The violinist has to be fourth, leaving the guitarist first.

146 **INNER CALM**

1   *Macabre*
2   *Requiem*
3   *Emperor*
4   (Sakari) Oramo
5   Modest
6   Staccato
7   Toccata
8   Tarrega
9   Gabetta
10 (Thomas) Tallis

147 **CODA**

Code: 1/L, 2/O, 3/V, 4/E, 5/C, 6/I, 7/D, 8/S, 9/R, 10/A, 11/K, 12/B, 13/T, 14/U, 15/W, 16/N, 17/M, 18/P, 19/Y, 20/X, 21/F, 22/G, 23/J, 24/H, 25/Q, 26/Z

Left to right and top to bottom of the grid:

ACROSS: ephemeral, love, laughter, Bartók, round, Borodin, box, theatre, largo, rhythm, fantasia, town, refreshed

DOWN: elaborate, overtures, polka, equinox, echo, ages, adoration, enjoyment, Boe, browses, brave, laze, star

Bluebeard's Castle by Bartók and *Prince Igor* by Borodin are the coded works.

148 **THREE TENORS**

Jonas plays Apollo.
Roberto plays Zeus.
Luciano plays Poseidon.

There are only six casting options involving three people going for three parts:

1   Jonas/Zeus, Roberto/Poseidon, Luciano/Apollo
2   Jonas/Zeus, Roberto/Apollo, Luciano/Poseidon
3   Jonas/Poseidon, Roberto/Apollo, Luciano/Zeus
4   Jonas/Poseidon, Roberto/Zeus, Luciano/Apollo
5   Jonas/Apollo, Roberto/Zeus, Luciano/Poseidon
6   Jonas/Apollo, Roberto/Poseidon, Luciano/Zeus

Statement A means option 1 won't happen.
Statement B means option 3 won't happen.
Statement C means option 4 won't happen.
Statement D means option 2 won't happen.
Statement E means option 6 won't happen.

Option 5 is the only one left!

149 **TRANSPOSING**

LAND OF HOPE AND GLORY,
MOTHER OF THE FREE,
HOW SHALL WE EXTOL THEE,
WHO ARE BORN OF THEE?

All letters transpose 21 places in the alphabet: A becomes V, B becomes W, C becomes X and so on.

150 **CRYPTIC**

Across

1 *Turandot*
7 Album
8 Theme
9 Co-star
10 *Fair*
12 *Rite*
14 *Fallen*
17 Liszt
18 Bream
19 Harpists

Down

1 Tubas
2 Rameau
3 Note
4 Opera
5 Barcarole
6 Metronome
11 Sambas
13 *Tosca*
15 Leeds
16 Stop

NOTES

NOTES

ALSO AVAILABLE FROM CLASSIC FM:

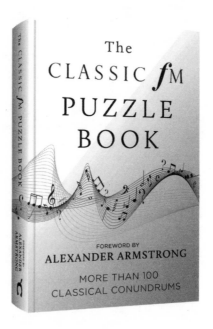

The Classic FM Puzzle Book (978-1-78840-138-8)

The Classic FM Puzzle Book 365 (978-1-78840-338-2)